British Railways Picto

First Generation Southern Region EMUs

Kevin Robertson

Ian Allan
PUBLISHING

First published 2005

ISBN (10) 0 7110 3087 1
ISBN (13) 978 0 7110 3087 9

Published by Ian Allan Publishing

an imprint of Ian Allan Publishing Ltd,
Hersham, Surrey KT12 4RG.
Printed in England by Ian Allan Printing Ltd,
Hersham, Surrey KT12 4RG.

Code: 0511/B

Visit the Ian Allan Publishing website at
www.ianallanpublishing.co.uk

Front cover: **No 7128 heads a line of 4-CEPs stored at Ardingly, 17 May 1959.** *R. C. Riley*

Back cover, top: **4-SUB No 4108 at Wimbledon, 22 June 1963.** *Colour-Rail*

Back cover, middle: **2-EPB 5712 at Mitcham, 13 March 1955.** *R. C. Riley*

Back cover, bottom: **4-REP 3010 at Wimbledon, 24 December 1968.** *Colour-Rail*

Title page: **Fully automatic couplings are tested at Aldershot on 5 August 1975 with a pair of 2-HAP units, Nos 6022 and 6023. Although successful, cost was the governing factor and the idea was not proceeded with at that time.** *R. E. Ruffell*

INTRODUCTION

Today, in the early years of the 21st century, we take rapid change for granted and the fact that so many of our machines and other items of equipment essential for everyday life are powered by the invisible power of electricity. Indeed, without electricity our present-day lifestyle would not exist.

Although the use of electric power is seen as the most modern and efficient form of propulsion for railways, the Southern third-rail electric multiple-unit (EMU) operation has remained largely unchanged from that introduced nearly a century ago, albeit of course, updated and modified both visually and technically. In fact, so little may have altered that the engineers and managers of the past, Szlumper and Walker to name but two, would still be able to readily identify the railway of today as similar to that which they knew themselves.

However, there have been developments over the years resulting in the system now in place today, the most visibly obvious being the appearance of the rolling stock with its sliding doors. No longer do commuters travel in LSWR 2-NOL or similar type units — some may say 'shame' — and even the latest trains depicted here, the CIGs, VEPs and REPs, are all now consigned to history. While it is possible to exercise nostalgia in this book to present a photographic record of these types, today's commuters rightly expect a differing form of accommodation

compared with that deemed suitable by earlier generations.

These words were being written just as the media was reporting that the UK railway system last year carried more passengers than at any time in the preceding 45 years, a commendable and remarkable achievement. Especially so, when it is considered the passenger route mileage is probably only two-thirds of that which existed 45 years ago.

Such facts have a bearing on what follows, for the purpose of this book is not to repeat again in detail the story of the Southern EMU from its earliest days to the present time, as for that the best reference is the excellent title *Southern Electric* by John Glover, a successor to G. T. Moody's earlier editions, published recently by Ian Allan Publishing.

Instead, and in agreement with the publisher, I have attempted to collate the scene as portrayed on what was the Southern Region in the period from 1948 through to about 1970, prior to the introduction of the new generation of BR designs of electric stock in the early 1970s. At the beginning of this period the old order could still be seen and is thus also represented in the book, in part. As time progressed, the pre-Grouping sets still running were withdrawn and eventually the building of Southern Railway-designed units came to an end but the next phase was really one of consolidation. BR Southern Region was seemingly dominated by various 4-SUB units, into which were slowly integrated the first of the British Railways standard

CONTENTS

Right: **A busy time at Dartford Junction on 18 April 1988. This is the connection for the routes from London through Greenwich, Bexleyheath and Sidcup. To the left, refurbished BR standard 4-EPB No 5610 leads the 17.52 Victoria to Gillingham via Sidcup and is held awaiting a path into Dartford station. In the centre, No 5621 of the same type brings up the rear of the 17.34 Gillingham to Charing Cross via Bexleyheath, while on the right, 2-EPB No 6275 forms the front portion of a Victoria to Dartford via Blackheath and Woolwich working.** *Brian Morrison*

designs, the new steel-bodied stock sometimes regarded as a new generation of stock (see table). Apart from these the only main-line units were those of Southern Railway origin in the form of the COR, PAN, CIT and PUL sets, and not forgetting, of course, the unique 'Brighton Belle' units.

It was not until the advent of the Kent Coast electrification scheme in the late 1950s that the first really new and, for the time, radical, main-line units began to appear with a design which would be perpetuated over more than a decade with the CIG and BIG units. This culminated in the 4-REPs for the Bournemouth line electrification in 1967. The REPs marked the end of building of the Mk1 style of rolling stock, and, ironically, were the first to be withdrawn, 20 years later. By contrast, a number of the CEP and CIG units from the 1950s and '60s soldiered on to the end of slam-door stock in 2005, although in differing uses from when they were introduced and having latterly survived on borrowed time.

Not to be forgotten are the ubiquitous 4-VEP units which began to appear in the mid-1960s with the design subsequently multiplied so that in the 1970s, at least, a casual observer might be forgiven for thinking many of the SR outer suburban services were formed of little else.

In life, of course, nothing is for ever, and on the railway, as elsewhere, managers and engineers are invariably considering the next move ahead. This we can witness today in the form of 'Networker Express', 'Desiro' and 'Electrostar' EMUs, but to return to this book, the subject dealt with here is the Southern Region in the period from Nationalisation to *circa* 1970 with the designs that were built and were operating during this period.

For many years I saw both steam and electric trains side by side, principally on the former South Western lines serving Waterloo, and at the time the naivety of youth meant I paid little heed to the changes affecting the electric units — the same sets were always there, or so it seemed, and in my ignorance I assumed they always would be. The same applied to the diesel multiple-units I witnessed, and which I regarded as interlopers to my beloved steam engines, but as time passes and the mind mellows one realises how important it is to recapture these scenes of one's youth.

In addition to the units themselves, the general railway scene of the period is depicted in this book. I know many readers, like myself, find such records fascinating and so the views have been selected, wherever possible, to incorporate the contemporary railway scene — the stations, the staff, ephemera and fashions — as well as simply depicting the EMUs. I hope it provides a wonderful sojourn in nostalgia. Railwaymen are often notoriously difficult to capture in typical pose, and a lot of what goes on behind the scenes has never been recorded, but one view in particular on this theme — that of the guard leaning out of the front window of a 4SUB to change the stencils on the indicator blinds — was too good to miss.

The Achilles' heel of the Southern electric service is that the main volume of traffic carried is compressed into just two brief periods per weekday. Ally this to the ever-increasing number of passengers, referred to earlier, and the fact that this increasing number is being carried on a network basically unaltered from a century ago, and small wonder then that the brains of several generations of managers, engineers and operators have tried, and perhaps not totally succeeded yet, to squeeze a proverbial quart into a pint pot. In many respects they have not obtained the recognition they deserve for their achievements. Greater line occupancy has been achieved due to more modern signalling (although perhaps the semaphore was more aesthetically pleasing), while trains now have greater seating capacity than ever before. Accommodation in earlier units, which may have appeared plain at the time of introduction, would now seem luxurious!

In the past, the new electric trains replacing steam-hauled suburban services were a victim of their own success as ever more people took the opportunity to travel, resulting in overcrowding. Today, similar problems face the railways, albeit in a more modern context.

However, this is an exercise in nostalgia with which I expect more than a few will identify. Some may even see some aspects of the subject in a different light to that which they may have done at the time.

For this work I have been extremely fortunate to have had access to some of the files of the late Denis Cullum. Denis worked for many years in the Rules and Records section of the Southern Railway and later the Southern Region and made it his duty to record the often minor changes to operations and procedure affecting both main-line and suburban, steam and electric services.

Some of his files affecting the last named are a rare glimpse into the behind-the-scenes operation of Southern electrics and it is with great pleasure that this information is published for the first time. I am deeply indebted to Neville Bridger for the loan of the material involved.

Kevin Robertson
July 2005

Left: **Tri-lingual information on the dangers of conductor rails at Dover Marine, 20 May 1967.** *Stephenson Locomotive Society*

BIBLIOGRAPHY

abc Southern Electrics (Ian Allan Publishing)
abc of British Electric Trains (1948) — G. Freeman Allen (Ian Allan Publishing)
The Southern Electric Story — Michael H. C. Baker (Silver Link)
British Multiple-units Volume 2: EPBs, Haps, Saps and Caps — Ashley Butlin (Coorlea)
Southern Electric — John Glover (Ian Allan Publishing)
British Rail Fleet Survey 10: Third Rail dc Electric Multiple-Units — Brian Haresnape and Alec Swain (Ian Allan Publishing)
Motive Power Recognition 2: EMUs — Colin J. Marsden (Ian Allan Publishing)
Southern Electric Multiple Units — Colin J. Marsden (Ian Allan Publishing)
Southern Electric — G. T. Moody (Ian Allan Publishing)
Southern Electrics: A View from the Past — Graham Waterer (Ian Allan Publishing)
The Southern Railway Handbook 1923–47 — David Wragg (Sutton Publishing)

EMU VEHICLE CLASSIFICATION CODES

BDMS	Battery driving motor second
BDTC	Battery driving trailer composite
BDTS	Battery driving trailer second
BUF	Buffet
DMBS	Driving motor brake second
DMS	Driving motor second
DMT	Driving motor third
DTBS	Driving trailer brake second
DTC	Driving trailer composite
DTS	Driving trailer second
DTSO	Driving trailer second open
DTT	Driving trailer third
DTLV	Driving trailer luggage van
FO	First open
GLV	Gatwick luggage van
GRI	Griddle
M	Motor van
MBLS	Motor buffet luggage standard
MBS	Motor brake second (MSB)
MBSO	Motor brake second open
MBT	Motor brake third (MTB)
MBTO	Motor brake third open
MCB	Motor composite brake
MLV	Motor luggage van
MS	Motor second
MSO	Motor second open
PAN	Pantry
PUL	Pullman
RB	Restaurant buffet
RMB	Restaurant miniature buffet
T	Trailer
TBC	Trailer brake composite
TBF	Trailer brake first
TBS	Trailer brake second
TC	Trailer composite
TCL	Trailer composite (lavatory)
TF	Trailer first
TK	Third corridor
TFH	Trailer first handbrake
TRB	Trailer buffet unclassified
TRBS	Trailer restaurant buffet second
TRSB	Trailer restaurant second buffet
TRT	Trailer restaurant third
TS	Trailer second
TSH	Trailer second handbrake
TSO	Trailer second open
TSW	Trailer standard wheelchair
TT	Trailer third
TU	Trailer unclassified

Above: **This is an interesting combination, recorded in Southern Railway days between Bromley South and Bickley. The eight-car train bound for Orpington consists of a NOL, No 1849, and a three 2-BIL units which were allocated on a weekly turnover basis.**

The well-known telegraphic codes such as NOL, LAV, SUB etc were introduced in 1932. With a frequent service provided on what was a congested and complicated network, the SR also introduced carriage side boards providing passengers with a guide to the train's destination — and perhaps more importantly, the route — and an example can be seen behind the driver's cab. These were withdrawn in 1939 and briefly restored in 1946, but only on the Central Section. *Ian Allan Library*

Right: **Timetable for the 1932 main-line electrification.**

SOUTHERN REGION EMU NUMBER SERIES

Unit no	Type	Origin	Formation	Introduced	Out of stock	Renumbered
Pre-Nationalisation stock						
Suburban stock						
989–1200	2	Steam stock ex-LBSC, LSW, SEC, and LBSC ac electric	T+T	1919–37	w/d 1941–8	
1201–84	3	LSW E1–84 (converted steam stock)	MTB+TC+MCB	1914–17	Aug 1942–8	4131–71/95–4234 series
1285–1310	3	New (Guildford & Dorking scheme)	MTB+TC+MTB	1925	Aug 1945–6	4300–25
1401–95	3	SEC steam	MTB+TC+MTB	1925–6	Aug 1946–9	4431–4594 series
1496–1524	3	New (Eastern section)	MTB+TC+MTB	1925	Aug 1945–6	4326–54
1525–34	3	SEC steam	MTB+TC+MTB	1925–6	Aug 1946–9	4431–4594 series
1579–99	3	LSW steam	MTB+TC+MTB	1932–7	Aug 1946–8	4411–29 series & 4518
1600	3	see 1801				
1601–30	3	SEC steam	MTB+TC+MTB	1927–8	Aug 1946–9	4431–4516 series & 4580/6–9
1631–57	3	LBSC steam	MTB+TC+MTB	1928–9	Aug 1947–8	4517–4614 series (10 units w/d 1948)
1658–1701	3	LSW steam	MTB+TC+MCB	1927–8	Aug 1947–9	4172–94/4235–50
1702–16	3	LBSC steam	MTB+TC+MCB	1928	Aug 1947–8	4517–4614 series
1717–72	3	LBSC ac electric	MTB+TC+MCB	1929–30	Aug 1947–9	4517–79 series
1773–85	3	LSW steam	MTB+TC+MCB	1930	Aug 1946–9	4517–4614 series
1786–90	3	LSW steam	MTB+TC+MTB	1930–1	Aug 1947	4406–9, 4190
1791–6	3	LSW steam	MTB+TC+MTB	1931	Aug 1948–9	4401–4614 series
1797–1801	3	LBSC steam	MTB+TC+MTB	1931–2	Aug 1948	4580–4614 series
(1801 renumbered 1600)						
1901–8	2-SL	LBSC ac electric	MTB+DTC	1909 (dc 1929)	w/d 1954	1801–8
1909–12	2-WIM	LBSC ac electric, steam 1912–29	MTB+DTT	1909 (dc 1930)	w/d 1954	1809–12

Note: the designations 2-SL and 2-WIM were not recognised in SR stock lists.

Unit no	Type	Origin	Formation	Introduced	Out of stock	Renumbered
Semi-fast stock (outer suburban and main line stopping)						
1813–62	2-NOL	steam	MTB+DTC	1934–5	w/d 1958–9	
1863–82	2-NOL	steam	MTB+DTC	1936	w/d 1956–8	
1883–90	2-NOL	steam	MTB+DTC	1936	w/d 1957–8	
1891–9/0,						
1901–20/54–71	2-BIL	new	MTB+DTC	1935–8	w/d 1969–71	2001–48
1921–53	4-LAV	new	MTB+TC+TC+MTB	1932	w/d 1968–9	2921–53
2049–2152	2-BIL	new	MTB+DTC	1935–8	w/d 1969–71	
2601–92	2-HAL	new	MTB+DTC	1939–40	w/d 1969–71	
2693–9	2-HAL	new (steel-bodied replacements)	MTB+DTC	1948	w/d 1969–71	
2700	2-HAL	MTB (new 1950)+DTC (new steel body on BIL underframe)		1954	disbanded 1968	
2954–5	4-LAV	new	MTB+TC+TC+MTB	1940	w/d 1968	
Express stock						
2001–20	6-PUL*	new	MTB+TC+TT+PUL+TC+MTB	1932	w/d 1965–6	3001–20
2021–37	6-PAN	new	MTB+TT+TF+PAN+TT+MTB	1935	w/d 1964–6	3021–37
2041–3	6-CIT*	new	MTB+TF+PUL+TF+TF+MTB	1931–2	w/d 1966	3041–3
2051–3	5-BEL	new (Pullman)	MTB+TF+TT+TF+MTB	1932	w/d 1973	3051–3

* new as '6-COR'

* new as '6-COR

Unit no	Type	Origin	Formation	Introduced	Out of stock	Renumbered
3041-50	6-COR	reformed 6-PUL & 6-PAN	MSB+TT+TC+TC#+TT+MSB	1965-6	w/d 1969	# ex-TF
3054-72	4-RES	new	MTB+FO+RTK+MTB	1937	reformed 1964-5 to 4-COR(N) or 4-PUL	
3054-9	4-PUL	reformed 4-RES	MTB+FO+PUL+MTB	1964	w/d 1965-6	
3073-85	4-BUF	new	MTB+FO+BUF+MTB	1938	w/d 1971	
3086-8	4-GRI	modified 4RES	MTB+FO+GRI+MTB	1961-2	w/d 1971	
3101-58	4-COR	new	MTB+TF+TC+MTB	1937-8/45/6	w/d 1971	
3159-68	4-COR(N)	reformed 4-RES	MTB+TF+TC+MTB	1965-6	w/d 1971	

Post-Nationalisation stock

(Augmented stock is Pre-Nationalisation mostly with an extra Post-Nationalisation trailer)

Augmented suburban stock and steel bodied suburban and semi-fast stock

Unit no	Type	Origin	Formation	Introduced	Out of stock	Renumbered
4001/2	4-DD	new	MTB+TT+TT+MTB	1949	w/d 1979	4901-2
4101-10	4-SUB	new	MTB+TT+TC*+MTB	1941-5	w/d 1972	
4111-30	4-SUB	new	MTB+TT+TC*+MTB	1946	w/d 1971-6	
4131-4250	4-SUB	augmented LSW (see above)	MTB+TC+TT+MTB	1942-9	w/d 1954-6	
4131/2	4-SUB	reforms from HAL MTB + SUB TT	MTB+TT+TT+MTB	1969	w/d 1971	
4250-7	4-SUB	spares ex-war/accident losses	MTB+TT+TT+MTB	1943-8	w/d 1949-56	
4277-99	4-SUB	new	MTB+TT+TT+MTB	1948-9	w/d 1981-3	
4300-54	4-SUB	augmented 1925 (see above)	MTB+TC+TT+MTB	1945-6	w/d 1959-62	
4355-77	4-SUB	new	MTB+TT+TT+MTB	1947-8	w/d 1972-6	
4378-87	4-SUB	new	MTB+TT+TT+MTB	1948	w/d 1972-6	
4401-4516	4-SUB	augmented SEC (see above)	MTB+TC+TT+MTB	1946-7	w/d 1949-56	
4501-18	4-SUB	augmented LBSC ac, reformed	MTB+TC+TT+MTB	1956-7	w/d 1959-60	
4517-94, 4601-14	4-SUB	augmented LSW/LBSC steam/ac	MTB+TC+TT+MTB	1946-7	w/d 1949-57	
4601-7	4-SUB	new	MTB+TT+TT+MTB	1950	w/d 1976	
4617-20	4-SUB	reforms	MTB+TT+TT+MTB	1972-6	w/d 1981-3	
4621-4754	4-SUB	new §	MTB+TT+TT+MTB	1949-51	w/d 1974-83	
5001-53	4-EPB	new §	MTB+TT+TT+MTB	1951-4	w/d or refurb 1987-94	
5101-5260	4-EPB	new §	MTB+TT+TT+MTB	1953-7	w/d or refurb 1987-94	
5301/2 (Part BR)	4-EPB	new BR MTB, SR TT	MBS+TS+TS+MBS	1960-1	w/d 1987, 1983	
5303-70 (BR)	4-EPB	new	MBS+TS+TS+MBS	1960-3	w/d 1983-5 or refurb (5601-30)	
5401-97	4-EPB	refurbished ex-5001-5260	MBS+TS+TS+MBS	1980-7	w/d 1991-4	
5501-30	4-EPB	reformed ex-5001-5260	MBS+TS+TS+MBS	1988	w/d 1990-1	
5601-30 (BR)	4-EPB	refurbished ex-5301-56	MBS+TS+TS+MBS	19xx	w/d 1993-5	compartment trailers
5601-36	2-HAP	new §	MBS+DTC	1957-9	refurbished	
5651-84	2-EPB	new §	MBS+DTS	1959	refurbished	63xx
5701-79 (BR)	2-EPB	new	MBS+DTS	1954-8	renumbered	6201-79 (some refurb: 6401-18)
5781-95 (BR)	2-EPB	new (ex-Tyneside 1963)	MBS+DTC (DTS on SR)	1954	renumbered	6281-93 (not 5794/5)
5800 (BR)	2-EPB	new	MBS+DTS	1960	disbanded 1964	
5901-51 (BR)	2-SAP	declassified 2HAP	MBS+DTS	1974	reverted to 60xx 1980	
6001-6173 (BR)	2-HAP	new	MBS+DTC	1957-63	renumbered or w/d	32xx/33xx/59xx 1982-5/91
6301-34 (SR)	2-EPB	refurbished	MBS+DTS	1982-5	w/d 1993-5	
6401-18 (BR)	2-EPB	refurbished	MBS+DTS	1985-7	w/d 1993-5	
3201-13 (BR)	4-CAP	paired 2-HAP then declassified	DTC+MBS+MBS+DTC	1982	w/d 1991-5	
3301-11/21-5/33 (BR) 4-CAP	paired 2-HAP then declassified	DTC+MBS+MBS+DTC	1982/91	w/d 1991-5		
4201	2-HAP	declassified 2-HAP	DTS+MBS	1988	reformed in 3333 1991	
4301-22	2-HAP	declassified 2-HAP	DTS+MBS	1987-8	w/d or reformed to 33xx 1991-5	

§ most vehicles new bodies on re-used underframes

Note: the description 'MTB' is derived from the SR description 'Motor third brake'. BR practice preferred 'Motor brake third', but the SR form continued to be used in underframe branding of SR-design vehicles.

BR Main line and semi-fast stock

Unit no	Type	Origin	Formation	Introduced	Out of stock	Renumbered
7001-22	4-BEP	new	DMBS+TC+RB+DMBS	1957-63	refurbished	2301-7
7031-48	4-BIG	new	DTC+MBS+RB+DTC	1965-6	renumbered	2101-12
7049-58	4-BIG	new	DTC+MBS+RB+DTC	1970	renumbered	2201-10
7101-7211	4-CEP	new	DMBS+TF+TS+DMBS	1956-63	refurbished	1500-1617/97-9
7301-7336	4-BIG	new	DTC+MBS+TS+DTC	1964-6	renumbered	1101-27
7337-7438	4-BIG	new	DTC+MBS+TS+DTC	1970-2	renumbered	1201-26/37-1300
1101-27 series	4-CIG	unrefurbished renumbered 4-CIG	DTC+MBS+TS+DTC	1986	refurbished	1701-36
1101-19	3-CEP	reformed ex-4-CEP	DMS+TBS+DMS	1998/9	w/d 2004	
1201-26/37-1300	4-CIG	unrefurbished renumbered 4CIG	DTC+MBS+TS+DTC	1986	refurbished	1801-91
1301-22	4-CIG	refurbished ex-1201 series (Greyhound)	DTC+MBS+TS+DTC	1989-92	w/d 2005	
1392-9	4-CIG	reformed 4-BIG inc CEP trailer	DTC+MBS+TS+DTC	1999	w/d 2005	
1401-11	3-COP	reduced ex-4-BIG then to 4-COP	DTS+MBS+(TS)+DTS	1997-8	w/d 2005	
1497-9	3-CIG	reduced ex-4-CIG	DTC+MBS+DTC	2004	2005/still in service	
1500-1617/97-9	4-CEP	refurbished	DMS+TBS+TC+DMS	1974/9-84	w/d 2005	
1701-62	4-CIG	refurbished ex-11xx, 21xx	DTC+MBS+TS+DTC	1982/9	renumbered 1901-8 w/d 2005	
1801-91	4-CIG	refurbished ex-1201 series	DTC+MBS+TS+DTC	1982	w/d 2005	
1901-8	4-CIG	Mk 6 power bogies	DTC+MBS+TS+DTC	1997	w/d 2004-5	
2001-4	8-DIG	4-CIG+4-BIG	as above CIG+BIG	1993	reverted to BIG and CIG 1997	
2101-12	4-BIG	unrefurbished renumbered	DTC+MBS+RB+DTC	1989	reformed to 1751-62	
2201-10	4-BIG	unrefurbished renumbered	DTC+MBS+RB+DTC	1982	some reformed to 1401-11	
2251-62	4-BIG	refurbished renumbered ex-4CIG	DTC+MBS+RB+DTC	1989	some reformed to 1392-9, 1406-8/10	
2301-7	4-CEP	ex-buffet units	DMS+TBS+TS+DMS	1983/4	reformed	
7701-7894	4-VEP	new	DTC+MBS+TS+DTC	1966-74	renumbered 3001-3194	
7901-12	4-VEG	VEP modified for Gatwick services	DTC+MBS+TS+DTC	1978	reverted to original 1979	
8001	8-VAB	Temporary tuffet unit	5-VEP (inc RMB)+3-VEP	1970	disbanded 1974	
3401-3594	4-VEP	refurbished ex-3001-3194	DTC+MBS+TS+DTC	1988-95	w/d 2005	
3801-12	4-VEP	renumbered ex 34xx/35xx	DTC+MBS+TS+DTC	1995	w/d 2005	
3821-42 series	4-VEP	reformed from 34xx and 39xx series	DTC+MBS+TS+DTC	2003	w/d 2005	
3901-19	4-VOP	declassified 4-VEP	DTS+MBS+TS+DTS	1999	w/d 2005	

Bournemouth electrification stock

Unit no	Type	Origin	Formation	Introduced	Out of stock	Renumbered
301-3	3-TC	new trailer sets ex-hauled stock	DTS+TBS+DTS	1966	reformed to 4-TC 429-31 1974	
401-28	4-TC	new trailer sets ex-hauled stock	DTS+TF+TBS+DTS	1966	renumbered 8001-28(1986)	
429-31	4-TC	reformed ex-3-TC	DTS+TF+TBS+DTS	1974	renumbered 8029-31	
432-4	4-TC	new trailer sets ex-hauled stock	DTS+TF+TBS+DTS	1974	renumbered 8032-4	
1901-4	4-REP	renumbered 4-REP	DMS+RB+DBS+DMS	1990/91	w/d 1991/2	
2001-15	4-REP	renumbered 4-REP	DMS+RB+DBS+DMS	1986/7	w/d 1987-9 on	
3001-15	4-REP	new (trailers ex-hauled stock)	DMS+RB+DBS+DMS	1966/74	renumbered 2001-15	
8001-34	4-TC	renumbered 4-TC	DTS+TF+TBS+DTS	1982	renumbered 84xx or w/d 1986	
84xx	4-TC	renumbered 4-TC	DTS+TF+TBS+DTS	1991		

PRE-GROUPING AND EARLY SOUTHERN RAILWAY SUBURBAN STOCK

Above: The Southern Railway and later British Railways Southern Region electric network owes its origins to the pioneering work undertaken by all three main pre-Grouping constituents, the SECR, LBSCR and LSWR. In so far as the LBSCR is concerned it would be tempting to dismiss its contribution as being limited, as the overhead electric system it introduced was later abandoned in favour of the 'third' rail. What may not be so widely known, however, is that the LBSCR was, in 1911, the instigator of the use of numbers as a headcode to identify trains on the newly electrified Crystal Palace line instead of the disc/lamp system. At the same time, an 'end destination' board was also fitted.

This identification system was developed from then on and in 1923 was widely adopted by the SR for all electric trains to the mutual advantage of both operating staff and passengers alike. Here, an ex-LBSCR eight-car suburban train shows the letter 'O' with a single dot above which enables it to be identified as a Victoria to Orpington or, after 1935, a Sevenoaks service running via Herne Hill and Petts Wood. It is seen passing through Bickley/Chislehurst Junctions. *W. V. Oxford*

Right: Another little known fact is that the LSWR did not utilise an Act of Parliament to sanction its new electric services and, instead, commenced operations under Board of Trade powers. The LSWR three-car electric units, two of which are seen here, had been rebuilt from former steam-hauled suburban bogie coaches. Unit No E29 leading, was one of 84 such units converted at Eastleigh in 1914-17, with accommodation varying between 172 and 190 passengers, depending on the lengths and layouts of the original vehicles. The service seen here operated on a circular route from Waterloo through Richmond, Hounslow and Brentford and then to Waterloo. The LSWR electric services were regular-interval operations insisted on by the LSWR General Manager, Sir Herbert Walker. *Ian Allan Library*

Left: The expansion of the electric system to Dorking and Guildford from 9 July 1925 naturally created a need for additional stock with construction of the units being shared by what was then the Metropolitan Carriage, Wagon & Finance Co (MCWFC) and the Birmingham Railway Carriage & Wagon Co (BRCW). Twenty-six of the 55 new three-coach units provided at this time were for these services and were numbered in the sequence 1285-1310. In this photograph, unit No 1291 runs through Clapham cutting. All this batch of units were augmented with an additional trailer coach in 1945-6 and were designated SUB, numbered 4300-4326. Most remained in service until the late 1950s.

The LSWR had intended to operate electric services earlier than the 1915 timetable and preparatory work commenced on the first power station at Durnsford Road as early as 1913. However, technical problems and then the impact of World War 1 caused a delay. In 1915 the GPO complained with regard to the electric service trials, claiming they interfered with its telephone lines. *Ian Allan Library*

Left: Following the introduction of the new three-car suburban units in 1925 on the Western and Eastern Sections, further units were converted from SECR steam stock and introduced on the Eastern Section in 1926. These were numbered 1496-1524 and 1525-1534. An example of this batch is seen here. This formation has yet to have its unit number applied; they were augmented to four-car units in 1945-6. The new units built for the Eastern Section, Nos 1496-1524, were similar to those ordered for the Western Section and were also constructed by MCWFC and BRCW. *Ian Allan Library*

Left: In the early 1940s the Southern Railway introduced its four-car suburban units. There were to be many variants but initially many incorporated existing stock. At Wimbledon the final days approach for 4-SUB unit No 4506, formed of former LBSCR/SR ac electric stock. It is bound for Chessington South. Figures for 1 January 1923 revealed the SR had a combined total of 434 electric vehicles of LSWR and LBSCR origin. By 1939, this figure had risen to 3,189 vehicles including trailer cars. *J. C. Beckett*

Right: **In early British Railways livery, with wording on the side where the former destination board would have been affixed, is three-coach unit No S1642, recorded at London Bridge on 24 March 1948 prior to working the 6.16pm Tattenham Corner and Caterham service via the East Croydon direct line. Sixteen of the 27 units were augmented in 1948-9 and renumbered in the 45xx/46xx series.** *J. H. Aston*

Right: **Driving motor coach No S8722S from unit No 4513, originating from LBSCR ac electric stock, is seen on what was clearly a hot August day in 1959.** *B. A. Haresnape*

Below: **1925-built unit No 4309, rebuilt from former LSWR suburban stock, is pictured at Victoria station on a Beckenham Junction service.** *Ian Allan Library*

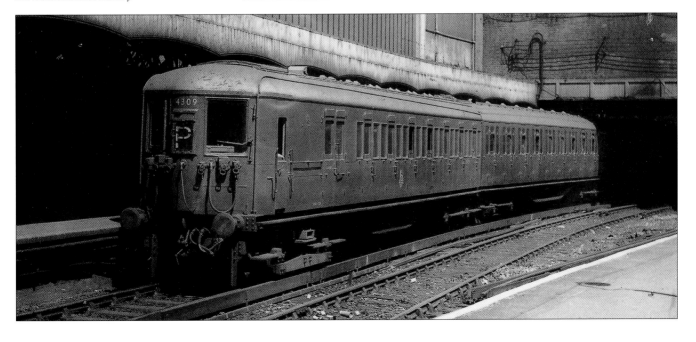

Left: **A former three-car unit strengthened to four cars by the addition of a Bulleid intermediate trailer, No 4338 with coach number S8441S leading, is seen at South Croydon on a London Bridge-Coulsdon North train.** *P. J. Sharpe*

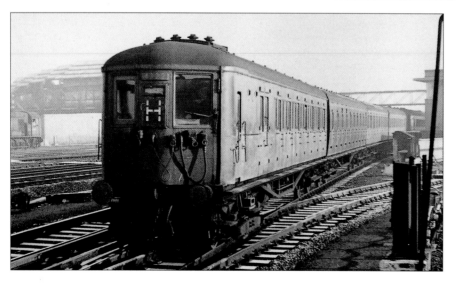

Above: **Busy times at Purley with augmented 4-SUB No 4314 of 1925 build, on a Brighton via Quarry excursion service — headcode '6' — with another EMU alongside and two BR-built units in the far background.** *Ian Allan Library*

Left: **A wintry scene at Clapham Junction — notice the distinctive signalbox spanning the running lines in the background, left. Augmented 4-SUB unit, No 4322, arrives on the Central Section side of the station.** *P. J. Sharpe*

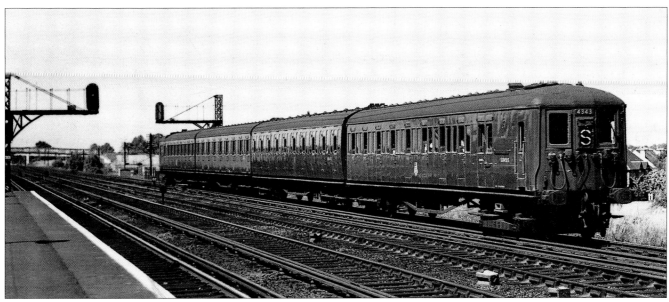

Above: **Also augmented from its original three-car formation with the addition of a Bulleid trailer, immediately after World War 2, was 4-SUB No 4343 on a Shepperton service. The Southern Railway lost a total of 93 vehicles as a result of enemy action, with a further 1,784 damaged during the war.** *G. M. Kichenside*

Right: **An advantage of standardisation was the ability to couple units together. Multiple-unit operation on the Southern was limited by the performance specification which required different designs but all 'SUB' units were compatible regardless of age or technical differences in control equipment, as seen here with unit No 4338 leading.** *P. J. Sharpe*

Left: **The basic front end design of early SR units and in particular the oblong cab window style could be seen well into the BR era. Another 4-SUB unit, this time No 4337, forms a Waterloo-bound service near Vauxhall on 2 July 1960.** *J. Courtney Haydon*

Left: **On 4 October 1959, Norbiton was affected by engineering work where the wrong line working at New Malden meant that services had to reverse. 4-SUB No 4306 is depicted having just transferred across to the down platform.** *J. H. Aston*

Left: **Pictured is motor brake composite No S9815S, with its body of LSWR 1905 origin on an underframe dating from 1921. It was derated to an all-third in 1941, in which form a number lasted until the 1950s, but not necessarily, it should be said, in particular comfort. There were definite advantages then to an austerity diet! No 9815 was in unit No 1780, augmented to unit 4573 and ended up in the second unit 4501, withdrawn in December 1959 as the last of the class in traffic.**

At the time of its suburban electrification, the LSWR was one of the first railway companies to abolish second class, having just first and third classes on its electric units. The introduction of electric units had seen LSWR passenger numbers more than double to 52.6 million per year in 1920, compared with those of steam-hauled services in 1913. A similar remarkable rise occurred between 1923 and 1939, although this time of course covering the whole of the SR, the figure rising from 236 million to 371 million. This was mainly attributable to the increase in electrified mileage, but was none the less remarkable when viewed against the backdrop of the depression of the 1930s. *G. M. Kichenside*

Left: **The era of British Railways was but six months old when this view was taken at Cannon Street on 9 June 1948 with 4-SUB No 4493 waiting to work the 11.34am to Dartford via Bexleyheath. For the moment at least, it is bereft of passengers while to the left is 'E1' class 4-4-0 No 1160 which had less than two years to survive, being withdrawn in January 1951.** *J. H. Aston*

Right: **This pair of driving motors from former 1925-built 4-SUBs Nos 4327 and 4354 was given unit No 4327 for operating purposes. After withdrawal from traffic in early 1960, they were used as match wagons for transferring trailers between Lancing Works and Gatwick sidings for storage. They were scrapped c1962. The single dot above the central panel used for the stencil code was used to modify the headcodes according to route and applied to certain services from Charing Cross, Cannon Street and Blackfriars on the Eastern Section, as well as some Central Division workings.** *Ian Allan Library*

Above: **Epsom Downs, on Derby Day, 4 June 1949 (the winner that year was 'Nimbus') with unit No 4558 formed of three cars of ac electric stock, built between 1914 and 1924, and a Bulleid trailer. The use of an oil tail lamp was standard at the time regardless of the electric technology in use and, indeed, it would be into the 1980s before this practice was finally abandoned, with the withdrawal of the last 4-SUB units. Tail lamps were abandoned on the Eastern Section in 1965, all its stock being EPB units by then.** *J. H. Aston*

Right: **No 4343 (original No 1513) was one of a batch of suburban three-car units which gained a Bulleid trailer when renumbered 4301-4354 in 1945-6. None of these units had corridors, all being of the basic single-compartment type and without toilet facilities of any kind.** *P. J. Sharpe*

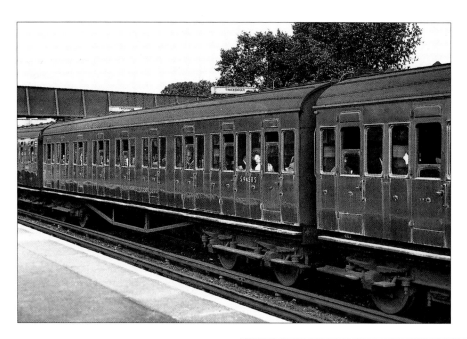

Left: **An original intermediate trailer in a 1925 suburban three-coach unit with one of the later all-steel additional trailers to the left. The last pre-1939 suburban units in passenger service, Nos 4308 and 4529, were eventually withdrawn from service in December 1961 and January 1962 respectively.** *G. M. Kichenside*

Right: **A close-up view of a similar vehicle to the previous picture, trailer car No S9595S built for the Eastern Section in 1925.** *Ian Allan Library*

Below: **Implementation of the SR's suburban rebuilding programme after Nationalisation involved the withdrawal of wooden-bodied units, the bodies of which were then broken up. This is the remains of motor brake third No 8264, from 4-SUB No S4446, the melancholy scene recorded at Lancing Works, west of Brighton on 5 September 1951.** *J. H. Aston*

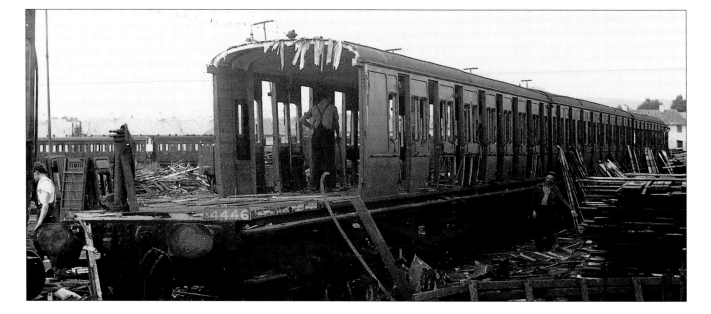

Motormen and Guards' Responsibilities

As the spread of electrification progressed, so consequently did the number of 'motormen' compared with steam drivers. Some staff, of course, preferred the clean working conditions, albeit of almost solitary confinement for much of the day. While this worked well most of the time, the fact there was now only one man in the cab soon led to the provision of a 'dead-man's' handle in the event of sudden illness affecting the driver. In steam days the fireman would invariably be able to bring the train to a halt. Electric traction was, of course, different. Accordingly, the Southern Railway (SR), in common it appears with the London, Midland & Scottish Railway, adopted the practice of giving guards instruction in the driving of electric trains when necessary. From a surviving SR document of 1929, it appears this practice dated back to London & South Western Railway days in 1915, and was originally intended to cover situations such as a motorman not reporting for duty. According to the 1929 document, though, this was never in fact put into practice and seemingly there was no occasion during the 12 months up to November 1929 that a guard was called upon to take over a train en route either.

The suggestion was then made that the weekly allowance of 2s 6d paid to guards in respect of this arrangement be abolished, so saving the Southern Railway no less than £3,314 per annum. (It was noted that different conditions applied on some Underground lines at the time where the normal line of promotion was from guard to motorman.) At the time, the matter was referred to the Sectional Council dealing with labour relations issues and it appears the allowance was discontinued from January 1930.

But this was not to be the end of the story, and after a period of a dozen years, in late December 1942, the National Union of Railwaymen (NUR) submitted an application for a 'special allowance' of 5s a week for an identical reason. Its case was put forward in detail outlining the additional responsibilities affecting the guard of an electric train, who could be required to assist the motorman on occasions. Unfortunately, perhaps, for the NUR but more particularly its members who would have benefited directly, the NUR's principal cases of the guard assisting the driver with short-circuiting bars, operating the controls for electric heating and the uncoupling of sets were all either dismissed as duties primarily of others, or the same or equivalent to a steam guard, or unlikely to occur except very rarely. The matter was then dismissed, although it appears it took no fewer than four years, through to 1946, to reach what was a perhaps the inevitable conclusion.

Above: **A Southern motorman. The advantage of working the electric sets was obvious — avoidance of the dirt associated with steam traction. Even so, motormen would have started their railway careers via the steam route before transferring across, some preferring the solitude.** *R. K. Blencowe*

Left: **Originally built for the Waterloo & City Railway in 1900, electric locomotive No 74S was transferred to Durnsford Road in 1915 where it was employed shunting coal wagons until the closure of the power station. Durnsford Road would continue in operation until the 1950s when, together with the main generating station at Deptford for the South Eastern lines, both were superseded by a £12 million investment approved by the Railway Executive in November 1950. The power station was not demolished until 1970.** *HMRS*

SOUTHERN RAILWAY SEMI-FAST AND EXPRESS STOCK

Left: Wrong line working at New Malden on 4 October 1959 when bridge works on the up lines meant all trains were being diverted. In the first view, 2-BIL (two-car lavatory units, lavatory in both coaches) No 2109 leads the 9am stopping service from Portsmouth & Southsea. *J. H. Aston*

Centre left: The 2-BILs, of which 152 were built, were introduced in 1935. With their side corridors to individual compartments, together with a lavatory in each coach, they proved extremely popular. Intended for both main-line working in multiple as well as branch-line duties they afforded a comfortable ride. Gatwick Airport station was rebuilt from Gatwick Racecourse and was brought into use on 28 May 1958, shortly before this photograph was taken on 30 August 1958. The modern style concrete design of the time makes the mechanical signalbox and vintage EMU appear slightly out of place. The train formed with 2-BIL No 2052 at the head of the 4.2pm Victoria to Littlehampton and Bognor Regis may have to run to Bognor reversing at Littlehampton. Behind it is an HAL which should cast off at Gatwick for return to Victoria on the next up train. *J. H. Aston*

Above right: At Ardingly on 9 September 1962 2-BIL No 2063 leads a four-car train forming the 4.16pm Horsted Keynes-Seaford service. By coincidence, the unit forming the other end of the train was No 2064. *J. H. Aston*

Below right: A 2-BIL unit, No 2071, is seen at Horsted Keynes forming the 6pm to Haywards Heath on 31 August 1957. There was only one platform line here that was electrified and the service ceased from 28 October 1963, exactly two years after the preserved Bluebell Railway had opened through to this station from Sheffield Park. *J. H. Aston*

Left: Sunshine and shadow at Waterloo (Main Line) on 16 June 1957 where 2-BIL No 2069 will shortly depart on the 12.34pm to Reading South service running on this occasion via the main line as far as Weybridge, then Chertsey and Virginia Water West Curve. This was necessitated by engineering works on that day. The headcode of '09' refers to a special working using this route. The headcode will be carried through to Reading South. *J. H. Aston*

Above: **An example of the 2-BIL use in multiple is depicted at Weybridge on 23 July 1966 with No 2057 bringing up the rear of the 11.30 Portsmouth & Southsea stopping service.** *Stephenson Locomotive Society*

Right: **Driving trailer coach No S12186S from 2-HAL No 2601 at Micheldever, c1957/8. The HAL units as originally built in 1939 ran from No 2601 to 2692. Originally they saw service on the Charing Cross lines to Maidstone and Gillingham, but when replaced on these routes by 2-HAPs in 1958 operated on all three divisions. The 'HAL' designation referred to one car only having lavatory provision.** *R. K. Blencowe*

Left: **The 2-HALs were slightly different in design to the 2-BILs in that the ends did not have the framing of the BILs, as one coach of the 2-HALs had only a side corridor and lavatory. When the HALs were working on the Western and Central Sections (as they all were from September 1959), they were interchangeable with the BILs, as here with No 2641 on the 15.57 Waterloo to Portsmouth photographed at Esher on 20 March 1966. The HALs were the first 9ft wide electric stock to be used on the Eastern Section and thus permitted the infamous six-a-side seating arrangement as the vehicles were wide enough at coach waist level. The bodies were constructed of steel sheet on a timber framework with wood and canvas; the cab structure was all steel.** *Stephenson Locomotive Society*

Right & centre right: **Seven 2-HAL units (Nos 2693-2699) were built as a direct replacement of rolling stock lost during the war. They had the same basic seating arrangements as the 1939 2-HALs, but were built to Bulleid's coach profile. The two vehicle types making up each set — driving motor brake third and driving trailer lavatory composite — are seen in these views of unit No S2699 and were recorded at Victoria on 26 March 1949 prior to working the 12.28pm Maidstone East service running via the Catford Loop. An eighth unit (No 2700) was formed from a Bulleid motor coach and a salvaged underframe with a new driving trailer body.** *J. H. Aston*

Left: **Thirty-three 4-LAV units (four-car units with one lavatory coach) were built in the period 1931/2 ready for the electrification of the line to Brighton. These were initially numbered 1921-1953 and renumbered 2921-2953 in 1937. A further two (2954-5 were built in 1940 with HAL-style ends. The 4-LAVs lasted well into the 1960s — most being withdrawn in 1968. In the 1940s two first class compartments in each unit were downgraded to seconds. They remained almost entirely on the duties for which they been intended, namely the slows and semi-fasts between the capital and Brighton and proved themselves well able to achieve a London–Brighton timing of just one hour when required. Unit No 2926 is seen on a slow service, possibly at Redhill. This particular unit was unique in that following an accident to one of its own motor brakes, it ran with a motor coach from 2-HAL No 2646. This was fitted with electro-pneumatic control gear.** *G. M. Kichenside*

Above: **An eight-car combination of LAV units is seen passing the old Gatwick Airport station on the Brighton line with No 2947 leading. Together with the PAN, PUL and BEL sets, these were the first really all-new electric units apart from some 1925 suburban units and ac electric stock, other previous stock having been conversions from steam-hauled vehicles.** *R. C. Riley*

Left: **Third class comfort in the compartment of brand-new coach No S10501S in 4-LAV No 2921 is shown in this official view. The moquette was a contemporary design, and a breakaway from conventional railway carriage materials. The general appearance is both inviting and restful.** *Ian Allan Library*

Right: **The 4-LAV sets provided a mixture of compartment and side corridor stock and access to the lavatories was limited. Side buffers were only used at the cab ends, the intermediate gear was single buffer and rubbing plate, while each set had four 275hp motors so giving a total horsepower of 1,100 for a four-coach unit. The 4-LAVs were able to accelerate rapidly from station stops and so be able to keep ahead of other traffic. For reasons of flexibility of operation, the SR later decided to concentrate on four-car combinations for subsequently built express units rather than six-car trains. This is 4-LAV corridor composite trailer No S12003S in unit No 2925.** *Ian Allan Library*

Left: **Brighton station on Saturday, 13 January 1968 sees 4-LAV No 2951 ready to depart for Victoria. The first two vehicles are identified as numbers S10562S and S12031S.** *Stephenson Locomotive Society*

Right: **Time for reflection at Burgess Hill as 4-LAV No 2947 awaits departure with the 14.47 Victoria to Brighton 'slow', on 19 September 1966. This unit has yet to receive any form of warning panel on the front.** *J. H. Aston*

Below: **Paused against a platform constructed of typical Southern concrete material, 4-LAV No 2931 waits with a London Bridge to Brighton train. The location is Redhill but this begs the question of why it is carrying a Quarry line headcode.** *P. J. Sharpe*

Left: **Alongside the associated paraphernalia of the modern-day electric railway, 4-LAV No 2931 is seen again, this time speeding away from the photographer, at Norwood Junction. It is hard to imagine that only just a generation ago trackside passes were available almost upon request.** *P. J. Sharpe*

Below: **All but two of the 4-LAV units were built in 1931/2, with a final pair, Nos 2954 and 2955, constructed at Eastleigh Works in 1939/40. Making up what was an eight-car train, unit No 2945 heads off on a London Bridge to Bognor Regis service running via Redhill and Horsham.** *P. J. Sharpe*

Left: **Complete with small warning panel, 4-LAV No 2930 is seen at Haywards Heath on a Victoria to Brighton semi-fast. The yellow bands denoting first class above some of the doors on the two centre coaches are clearly visible.** *Carl Symes*

Left: **A final view of a LAV unit: this time No 2951 leads an eight-car formation departing from Haywards Heath with the 10.45 from Victoria for Brighton on 27 August 1967. Most of the SR-built units lasted until withdrawn in 1968 when replaced by the influx of BR-built VEP units.** *John Scrace*

Below: **To many the front end of the PAN and CIT sets presented a businesslike appearance, due no doubt to the provision of almost square windows under the swept-down cab roof dome, as seen on 6-PAN unit No 3036.** *Ian Allan Library*

Below: **6-CIT unit No 3043 is seen at London Bridge on 9 April 1949 forming the 1.5pm (Saturdays only) service to Brighton.** *J. H. Aston*

Left: The former 6-CIT units — originally with three first-class trailers — were designated 6-PUL by the SR in 1946, meaning a six-car formation including a single Pullman vehicle. Here, No 3004 enters Lewes with the headcode describing a Victoria to Ore service via the Quarry line and Eastbourne. Heavy batteries within the sets afforded 30 minutes of emergency lighting if required. *P. J. Sharpe*

Right: A 12-coach formation on the 14.25 Victoria-Littlehampton service on 7 August 1965, with 6-PUL No 3005 leading. The building of the motor coaches of these sets was outsourced to Metropolitan-Cammell and the Birmingham Railway Carriage & Wagon Co, while the Pullman cars within the sets were all built by Metro-Cammell. In later years, further contracting out of electric stock construction took place. To the rear there is a 6-PAN unit, which, as the name implies, included a small pantry car capable of serving only limited meals. Passengers requiring a full meal service had to take care to join the correct portion of the train as there were no gangways between the units. There was variation in window design between the PUL and PAN sets, the latter having the option in the motor brake saloons for the top to slide open for ventilation, a feature which became standard on all SR, BR(S) and BR Mk 1 main-line stock until the 1970s. *John Scrace*

Left: Testing the seats is in progress at Eastleigh carriage works in November 1932 for 6-COR stock being built for the Brighton Line electrification. A 6ft compartment width was regarded by the Southern as the standard for third-class passenger comfort. This view persisted until the 1980s when British Rail designers, notwithstanding the fact that the population is acknowledged to be getting physically bigger, reduced this width in obedience to Ministry of Transport cost rules.
Ian Allan Library

Right: 'Six + six', two PAN/PUL units coupled together. Each driving vehicle was a third class saloon or 'open' coach, which was followed by a trailer third and a trailer first. After this came either the Pullman or pantry vehicle followed by another trailer composite third (in the PUL) or a trailer (in the PAN) and, at the opposite end, a third open driving vehicle. These units remained in service in these formations until 1963/4. Their replacements, York-built CIG and BIG units, had only buffet and snack catering facilities, following a re-evaluation of anticipated customer demand.
R. K. Blencowe

Centre right: Unit No 3053, leading a 10-coach formation comprising two of the three 5-BEL units (five-coach all-Pullman unit) used almost exclusively on the 'Brighton Belle' service between Victoria and the Sussex coast. (In the 1948 summer timetable there was a Victoria-Eastbourne Pullman service using one of these units.) Originally numbered 2051-2053, '1000' was added to their identification by the Southern Railway in Jan 1937. For many years the regular clientele made it much like a travelling club and the trains were well patronised not only by business folk but also stars of stage and screen, a number of whom had homes on the Sussex coast. Due to the age of the vehicles and there being no financial case for a comparable replacement, the service came to an end in 1972, with the only other multiple-unit Pullman services to run in the UK, the Blue Pullmans, bowing out the following year. *L. G. Marshall*

Lower right: Possibly the best known, and from the enthusiasts' perspective, most sadly missed units of the SR electric era are the 4-COR, 4-RES and 4-BUF units (four-coach units, corridor throughout; with restaurant or buffet facilities). Introduced from 1937 onwards (the inaugural train from Portsmouth was operated with unit No 3058), with the electrification of the 'Portsmouth Direct' line, the sets displayed a forward approach which would be developed over time, namely the provision of a corridor connection at the front end. While in no way did this enhance the aesthetics of the trains, the simple removal of the headcode to the position of the offside cab front window immediately gave a lopsided impression which was, for whatever reason, universally acclaimed. Unintentionally, the SR had also scored through the appearance of the units, as the new trains quickly took on the nickname 'Nelsons', although here the connection was with the one-eyed admiral of the same name and not the 'Lord Nelson' class steam locomotives also running on the Southern at that time. Here, 4-COR No 3120 is seen in May 1938, probably at Fratton, at this early stage only fitted with multiple-unit jumper connections to one side. The duplicate jumper sets were provided in the 1938 (Portsmouth No 2) stock from new and the 1937 units were then altered. *Southern Railway*

Above: The catering facilities within one of the 4-RES sets. Clearly, it was anticipated there would be thirsty passengers judging by the number of glasses overhead! There were originally 19 with restaurant facilities, 13 with buffet facilities and 55 4-CORs with seating only. During World War 2 some restaurant cars were lost so from 1946 the fleet was 58 COR, 16 RES and 13 BUF — until further alterations to No 3072 and the Griddle conversions of the 1960s when the restaurant facilities were reduced and eventually phased out. *Southern Railway*

Above: Leading an eight-car formation near Dorking North on a Bognor Regis and Portsmouth to Victoria service is 4-COR No 3114. For the Portsmouth electrification scheme power supplies were taken from the National Grid on a basic ring-main system fed from sub-stations which were in turn remotely controlled from central control rooms. *David Sellman*

Left: The location is unmistakably Clapham Junction and seen from ground level one cannot fail to be impressed with the 4-COR units. It will be seen that this is a 12-car formation which was the standard for most Portsmouth fast services. This particular train is on a service from Waterloo on 14 April 1949 and comprises two 4-COR and one 4-RES set. In recent times it has been suggested that with just 900hp available per four vehicles, the COR/BUF/RES units were underpowered. In later years the REP sets could only muster 3,200hp for a 12-coach train, just a 500hp difference from the CORs. *C. C. B. Herbert*

Right: **A trailer composite in a 4-RES set seen in BR days showing the side buffers fitted to intermediate vehicles which were intended to reduce the jolts suffered by passengers at speed, compared with the standard centre-buffer suburban stock. Aside from the obvious inclusion of a restaurant car, the internal fittings and décor were similar to that in the 4-CORs. Towards the end of their life some 4-RES units were reformed with a Pullman car from withdrawn PULs.** *P. J. Sharpe*

Left: **Although the 4-CORs were built to use stencil headcodes, they were converted to roller blind headcodes in the early 1960s. No 3117 awaits the headcode blind to be set for the next journey.** *Ian Allan Library*

Below: **Further innovation in BR days is demonstrated by 4-RES unit No 3072 on a test trip between Lancing, Redhill and Brighton on 2 November 1956, formed with Pullman car Brenda. This was the testing of modified bogies on the Pullman car with the intention that this modification would be applied to all the coaches then running in the 6-PUL units as the bogies designed for the PUL/BEL units were renowned for poor riding. The bogies were modified at Peckham Rye shops between December 1956 and November 1958. The formation is seen leaving Redhill on the return part of the journey. Note also the reversed headcode plate.** *Ronald S. Williams*

Above: **In the early 1960s 4-COR No 3126 leads a 12-car formation on the fast line at Byfleet & New Haw with a Portsmouth service.** *John H. Bird*

Right: **A cold January day in 1966, and the 12.20 Portsmouth Harbour to Waterloo service is captured leaving Portsmouth & Southsea station. The yellow panel on the lower half of the 4-COR's corridor screen was a feature of this period although for the present at least, the basic green livery remained.** *E. Thomas*

Left: **Mitcham Junction — the route from Merton Park and Wimbledon coming in from the left — with a down Portsmouth and Bognor Regis service from Victoria rounding the curve. The roofboards will be noted. While, as previously stated, the 4-COR units were popular with enthusiasts, the public would sometimes complain they rocked from side to side — perhaps in time with their nautical connections!** *David Sellman*

Left: **Busy times at Havant Junction in March 1968, just east of Havant station and the location of the connection between the 'Portsmouth Direct' and the coast lines — that to Chichester going straight ahead. Leading two other corridor sets bound for Portsmouth is 4-COR No 3121 in early blue livery with a small yellow panel while a 2-HAL unit from the 2693-2699 batch heads north across the same junction destined for Petersfield and Guildford.** *John H. Bird*

Right: **The afternoon sun catches the side of very clean 4-COR No 3125, on what appears to have been a hot afternoon. This was of course long before the days of air conditioning and drivers would also suffer as the cabs of these units could become very hot.** *P. J. Sharpe*

Below: **Unit No 3153 leans to the curve at Vauxhall — the main-line station for The Oval cricket ground — on its way to Portsmouth. Only occasionally did the units stray from their original haunts on the Portsmouth route and the Bognor–Brighton main line, with Eastbourne and Hastings excursions and Gillingham trips in the 1940s and 1950s, and for many years it was unusual to see a unit running singly. This is the 12.50pm Waterloo to Portsmouth Harbour on 21 June 1960.** *John Scrace*

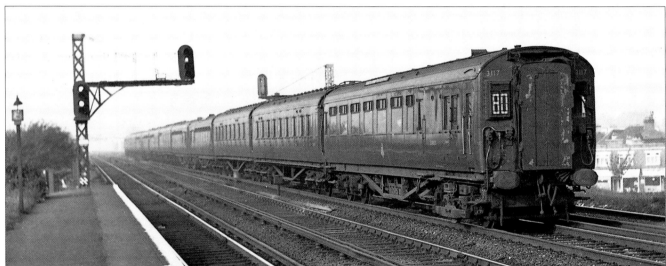

Above left: **A 4-COR + 4-RES + 4-COR formation with No 3143 leading is on the approach to Raynes Park having been diverted via Horsham due to engineering work near Guildford, on 27 October 1957. These were the first Southern EMUs in which a gangway was provided between the units. The advantage of course was that all passengers could avail themselves of a single catering vehicle and the guard and travelling inspector could access the whole train. This was in contrast to the Southern Region's 1950s-built Hastings line DEMU stock which had no end corridor connections.**
J. N. Faulkner

Centre left: **Raynes Park is passed at speed with 4-COR No 3117 leading a standard 12-coach Portsmouth line formation. Note on the platform, left, the eight-car stop sign — like the train, this style of stop sign is now consigned to history.** *P. J. Sharpe*

Below left: **Horsham did not only see the 4-COR units on diversions as No 3104 forms the regular 9.18am Victoria to Bognor Regis and Portsmouth service, dividing at Barnham, on 10 May 1959. The headgear worn by the motorman is, it appears, slightly unusual.** *John Scrace*

Above: **A 4-COR motor brake third saloon, No S11228S, of unit No 3155, is recorded at Havant.** *P. J. Sharpe*

Centre right: **London Waterloo-bound, and nonstop through Wimbledon, is a 12-car formation led by 4-COR No 3119.** *P. J. Sharpe*

Lower right: **London Bridge on 9 April 1949 with 4-COR No 3111 leading the 1.24pm service to Littlehampton routed via the Quarry line and Worthing. Had the SR been able to continue as an independent company then there were plans for an extension of electrification and dieselisation to cover all lines east of Portsmouth by the end of the 1950s.** *J. H. Aston*

Left: **Good for revenue perhaps, but not for public relations: standing passengers in the corridor of trailer composite No S11812S of 4-COR No 3122. The date is not known but the location is Havant, east of Portsmouth.**
G. M. Kichenside

4-COR Set Route Indicators

Any organisation, such as a railway company, generates a large amount of paperwork including records, files, charts, suggestions, notes and the like. Most is required for a certain period and is then cast aside to disappear as waste paper. It would have been impossible to retain everything although it is fortunate so much railway paperwork has been saved and now reposes in collections including the National Archive (Kew), and the National Railway Museum.

Apart from that, what escaped the skip was often down to a clerk or a manager stuffing papers away perhaps in a cupboard, regarding them as potentially 'interesting' and not wanting to see someone's work discarded without further thought.

This was the case with the late Denis Cullum, who for many years worked in the Rules and Records section of the Southern Region. Realising the significance of the papers he had access to, Denis ensured they were not destroyed and instead collated these items which covered a vast number of subjects, including details of various routes, signalling and motive power.

In the latter category were three small files relating to EMUs. The information contained therein would otherwise have been lost, and certainly long forgotten.

The first of these refers to the detail fittings on what would become the 4-COR sets. The initial meeting on the subject was held at Eastleigh on 26 March 1936. In the chair was E. A. W. Turbett of the CME Department accompanied by eight other men representing the CME, Electrical and Traffic departments. For the meeting, a model of the 'nose end' and driver's cab

arrangements of a 4-COR had been provided, although from reading the various reports this appears to have been a model built to full size!

Even at this stage the idea of an offset route indicator was being considered although one of the conclusions of the meeting was that, as proposed, the position of the indicator box was too high from the floor level of the coach. It was therefore decided to lower this so that the top of the box would be level with the top of the driver's window on the opposite side of the coach. (An alternative still seemingly under consideration at this time was a central indicator above the gangway, but this was later rejected.)

At the same meeting it was suggested that in place of folding doors to the gangway, a roller shutter be provided. One member of the group expressed doubt that this would be satisfactory in service and followed up with the intriguing statement: '. . . there are vehicles already in service with roller shutters . . .' (Later, this was stated to be on just one vehicle, No 5630, and it appears it was the CME himself, R. E. L. Maunsell, who was against the shutter principle, possibly due to vibration caused by air pressure when running at speed with the 'engine propelling'.)

As first presented the front gangway had a loose fabric covering, purely for aesthetic purposes for when the gangway was folded back, but this was changed to a corrugated material.

Due to limited space consequent upon having a corridor connection, the new Portsmouth line stock would be the first to be fitted with a handbrake elsewhere than in the driver's cab, and accordingly

it was stated it was to be in the guard's compartment. (The Traffic Department representative was satisfied with this arrangement.) One upshot, though, of moving the handbrake was what would happen should a failure of the power brake occur and the stock need to be moved to a convenient station or depot. For this event, the fixed glass panel separating the driver and guard's compartments would be provided with a hinged flap to enable communication when necessary.

The following week, a further meeting was held at Eastleigh, at which the position of the indicator on the model was adjusted, as discussed. Some delegates were of the opinion that, for ease of visibility from the nearside of the vehicle, the indicator should be further forward and in line with the face of the gangway. It was pointed out that the disadvantage of this was that the motorman would have to lean forward too much when changing the stencils and the position was also thought to be unsuitable as far as appearance was concerned.

Some years later, on 29 November 1948, a single sheet of paper refers to a month's trial of a roller blind on a brand-new 4-SUB unit, No 4355. In this form the set had been inspected at Charing Cross on 19 July. It was reported that signalmen had commented favourably as the indication was more clearly seen. The cost of the fitting was estimated at just £15 per unit, but £450 would be saved annually in maintenance of the stencils then in use. A general change certainly took place, but only with regard to newly built stock after that time, and stencils remained in use on older stock until at least the end of the 1970s.

Right: **Swinging around Witley curve between Haslemere and Guildford, a 12-coach rake including in the centre a 4-BUF unit with 4-COR No 3154 trailing, disappears in the direction of Waterloo in July 1966. Because of the ever-pressing need for as much accommodation as possible during World War 2, the buffet cars in 4-BUFs Nos 3073-85 were stored for much of the duration of the war because they had little useful passenger space suitable for war-time conditions. The catering cars in 4-RES Nos 3054-72 remained in their units with the kitchens locked and all the seating (which was more suitable) in use.** *John Goss*

Left: **Towards the end of their careers some 4-CORs and 4-BUFs received the all-over blue livery with full yellow ends, although they did not subsequently get the blue/grey livery when the other main-line stock did. It is doubtful if anyone felt this was an improvement to their appearance and if anything, it served to emphasise their advancing years. Set No 3103 pauses at Worthing on 19 July 1971 with the 21.45 Brighton to Littlehampton service.**
Paul Clark

Below: **The unmistakable scene of Lewes, although already in the throes of track and signal rationalisation, with 4-COR No 3141 on the 11.14 Brighton to Lewes service seen from the signalbox steps, 16 September 1972.** *J. H. Aston*

STEEL-BODIED SUBURBAN AND SEMI-FAST STOCK

Left: **Thirty four-car suburban units were ordered in November 1938 for construction in 1939/40. Unit No 4101 was completed in 1941 and designated 4-SUB in 1942. Nos 4102-10 were completed in 1942-5. They were to a new design with steel side panels but wooden roofs. Known as the 'Sheba' stock, total capacity was an amazing 468 persons in six-a-side seating. Used initially on the Victoria–Orpington line and later throughout the suburbs, they were an attempt to cope with the sardine-type crush found during the morning and evening peak-hour services. After No 4110 was built, the design was changed. Set No 4103 arrives at Purley Oaks on a Victoria and Coulsdon North service.** *P. J. Sharpe*

Above: **Another 4-SUB of the same batch, this time No 4105, passes the signalbox at Shortlands with a Sevenoaks to Holborn Viaduct service, running via the Catford Loop. Excluding the infamous double-deck units, these particular 4-SUBs represented the maximum seating capacity in any single SR unit with opposing passengers literally having to knock knees with their neighbours. For those in the know it was preferable to find one of the intended first class compartments that had never been used as such and had third-class upholstery.** *R. C. Riley*

Left: **The first 4-SUB unit of this batch, No 4101, is seen at Horsham on 3 August 1972.** *John Scrace*

Bottom right: **No S11333, a brand-new motor brake third saloon for 4-SUB unit No 4637 is at Eastleigh Carriage Works on 17 September 1949. This design would become the basis for the standard type of unit for suburban working over the next four decades. Among other items, the electric shoe gear has yet to be fitted, which would be done at Selhurst as delivery would be via non-electrified lines.** *J. H. Aston*

Left: **A further batch of 4-SUBs, unit numbers 4111–4120, was constructed in 1946. In a departure from previous practice, they were built with all-steel bodies. This time the number of compartments was reduced by one in each coach compared with Nos 4101-10 so that the total capacity was a mere 420 in a four-car unit. No 4118 is soon to depart from Waterloo with the 5.59pm to Hampton Court on 22 July 1947. The apparently admiring group on the opposite platform are probably looking at the photographer.** *J. H. Aston*

Below: **Postwar 4-SUB No S4369 at London Bridge on 10 March 1948 forms the 4pm Cannon Street-Plumstead circular service. Evidence of new ownership is present on the front of the unit, although lettering in this position did not last for long.** *J. H. Aston*

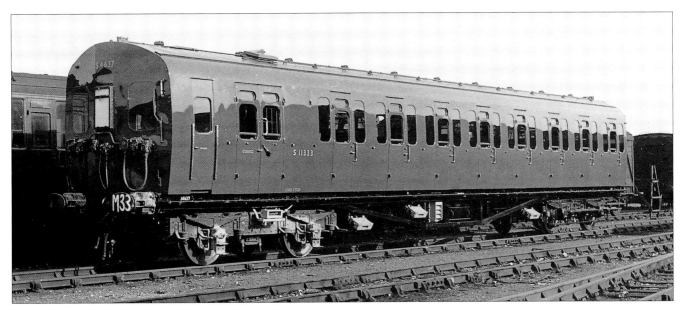

Above: **Door fitting at Eastleigh on a suburban unit. Although undated, this photograph shows a composite, almost certainly No 11500 for unit No 4130, built in September 1946.** *Ian Allan Library*

Right: **'Unwrapped and out of the packet' but still with a long way to go, the basic shell of what will later become part of a 4-SUB unit is seen at Eastleigh in October 1948. At this time these units were still being built with new steel bodies on new underframes but from 1949 to 1959, most 'new' suburban stock had new steel bodies on reconditioned underframes. The last occasion old underframes were used was in 1959 when a batch of 2-EPB units, Nos 5651-5684, was built on those of former 2-NOLs.** *J. H. Aston*

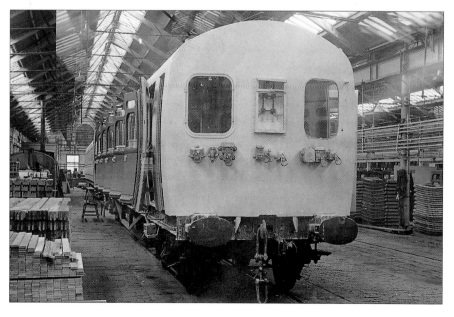

Left: **Fitting out at Eastleigh in October 1948, when replacement and repairs were hampered by a general shortage of steel and, especially at this time, electrical equipment.** *J. H. Aston*

Above: **To the same 4-SUB design, No 4720 is complete and in operation. The location is New Cross Gate and the service is one from London Bridge to Epsom Downs on 13 May 1959. To the right is an 'F' stock LU electric unit, on part of the East London Line, and also BR Standard Class 4 tank No 80154.** *J. H. Aston*

Centre right: **Frequent services were the policy of the Southern, both as Railway and Region. The rebuilt 1949-51 4-SUB units had a seating capacity of 386 based on the motor coaches having eight-bay saloons and the trailers having 10-bay saloons or 10 compartments. The requirement for the railway to carry countless thousands during a limited peak-hour period morning and evening gave rise to a publicity campaign in the 1960s to stagger working times. In that respect the railway was requesting employers to adopt staggered company working hours, but sadly, such requests generally fell on deaf ears. Although working hours may be more flexible today, the rush-hour peaks still remain, decades later. Set No 4114 passes Mitcham Junction signalbox.** *Ian Allan Library*

Lower right: **Although the all-compartment stock of 1946 (Nos 4111-20) was identical in so far as the motor coaches were concerned, 4-SUBs Nos 4355 through to 4363 had two 10-compartment intermediate vehicles and a seating capacity of 432 persons. No 4356 is depicted in motion near Clapham Junction, on a Guildford via Epsom stopping service.** *P. J. Sharpe*

Left: **The Bulleid influence at Waterloo. The unmistakable side profile of the 4-SUB electric set contrasts sharply with what was a rather uninspiring front end. Set No 4115 is recorded on 30 July 1949 leaving with a Waterloo to Waterloo circular service via Teddington. To the left is a Bulleid Pacific.** *C. C. B. Herbert*

Left: **Two variants of 4-SUB units speeding away from Norwood Junction, that trailed by No 4630 showing how, over the years, the body width had been increased from 8ft until 1925, to 9ft from that year and then to 9ft 3in from 1941. By 1951, the Southern Region had a total of 720 route miles electrified and operated 3,289 electric train vehicles and was then by far the largest operator of EMUs on British Railways. Interestingly, the next largest was the LMR Euston-Watford service which was running on a fourth-rail system at 630V dc.** *P. J. Sharpe*

Left: **Norbiton on 10 May 1959 sees 4-SUB No 4738. Normally, it would have arrived displaying stencilled headcode '62', which was for trains from Waterloo to Kingston via Twickenham, but due to engineering works a reversal has taken place and the blank rear panel is shown. A little known fact is that stations on the LSWR electric network in 1915-17 were lit by electricity from the conductor rail. The justification was that the image of the electric service would suffer if the then modern technology was associated with a location lit by oil or gas.** *J. H. Aston*

Above: **On 28 February 1970 one of the last SR-type 4-SUB units built, No 4743, takes Hampton Court Junction flyover, just west of Surbiton, this also being the point of divergence for the 'new line' to Guildford (left under the flyover). The last 4-SUB unit built was No 4754.** *Ian Allan Library*

Right: **Nearing the end of its days at Selhurst on 26 September 1983, 4-SUB No 4629 is in company with Departmental unit No 022.** *John Scrace*

Below: **Away from the metropolis and heading through Kent, 4-SUB No 4647 approaches Knockholt on a Charing Cross to Sevenoaks service, 10 May 1952.** *R. E. Vincent*

Left: **In fresh green livery, 4-SUB No 4744 catches the late afternoon sunshine.** *P. J. Sharpe*

Right: **Platform 8 at Wimbledon with 4-SUB No 4670 on a Waterloo to Shepperton service. It is just possible to glimpse contemporary District Line tube stock in the background, left.** *P. J. Sharpe*

Below: **4-SUB No 4670. Excluding wartime restrictions, the speed limit in the suburban stock area, and for suburban stock anywhere, was set at 60mph, while express stock on the Brighton and Portsmouth lines was limited to 75mph. Even so, only BR Standard express and semi-fast stock were fitted with speedometers, and then only from 1971.** *P. J. Sharpe*

Left: With electric floor-level heating provided within the vehicles, it was not uncommon for passengers to doze off on such occasions as this cold and frosty morning! Believed to be on a Central Section service (Victoria-Epsom-Guildford) is 4-SUB No 4696. *P. J. Sharpe*

Below: Yellow warning panels were added to units from c1963. Set No 4704 at Clapham Junction on the former Brighton lines working a Victoria to Sutton service via Streatham Common and West Croydon on 29 June 1967. *John H. Bird*

Below: Chessington South station is seen on 17 February 1968 with 4-SUB No 4680 working the 15.35 to Waterloo. Opened on 29 May 1939, the intention had been for the line to be extended through to Ashtead. The two Chessington stations were originally intended to be suffixed 'Court' and 'Grange'. Due to changes in town planning policies and the very high cost of building the line, it was never completed. In the event, a simple 'North' and 'South' were used to distinguish the stations. *Stephenson Locomotive Society*

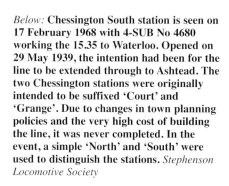

Above left: **Viewed from the opposite end of Chessington South station on the same day, 4-SUB No 4702 forms the 16.05 to Waterloo. The Chessington branch has benefited from a regular-interval service since the time of opening through to the present day.** *Stephenson Locomotive Society*

Above: **A scene re-enacted thousands of times and yet rarely captured on film: changing the headcode of a 4-SUB as seen at Coulsdon North on Saturday, 14 August 1982 with No 4749. The train was a special chartered by the Southern Electric Group and was operating the 'Mary-go-Round' railtour. Coulsdon North was closed permanently in 1982.** *David Brown*

Centre left: **Another stopping place on the same line, and consequently with the same style of architecture, is Tolworth, where 4-SUB No 4660 has arrived and awaits departure with the 15.05 to Waterloo on 16 March 1968.** *Stephenson Locomotive Society*

Left: **A Haslemere to Waterloo train with 4-SUB No 4658 is seen at Godalming in leafy Surrey on Monday, 9 June 1969.** *Stephenson Locomotive Society*

Right: **Bulleid's folly, the 4DD double-deck unit of 1949, No 4001, recorded when brand new. In fairness it must be stated that the concept of the trains — alternate low and high compartments rather than double-deck in the true sense of the word — was the product of an able and fertile brain. Sadly, what worked well on paper did not transmit well to practice and apart from the original two sets built, the design was not perpetuated.** *H. M. Madgwick*

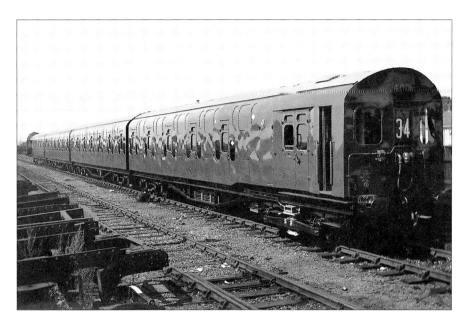

Below: **The double-deck units in service are leaving Cannon Street on 12 June 1959. Restrictions due to the loading gauge meant the trains had to be limited in operations to the route between Charing Cross/Cannon Street and Gravesend. Accordingly, although in regular commuter peak use, most of the suburban electric system never saw them.** *R. C. Riley*

Above: **In order to accommodate the double-deck body within the loading gauge, the bogie wheels had to be smaller than standard, which led to the temporary withdrawal of the sets almost immediately they had begun operating due to cracks being found. The matter was soon resolved and they continued to operate for over two decades until withdrawn in 1971, although the decision not to multiply the type had been made as early as December 1950. This and the next detail view show No 4901 (previously No 4001) at Plumstead on 7 October 1971.** *John Scrace*

Above: **Where the double-deck design had not perhaps taken into account of the practicalities was in the additional time taken to load and empty the trains, while passengers could also feel trapped within the upper compartments. For these reasons the design was never multiplied. Fifty years on, at least one operator of today's privatised rail network is showing an interest in a similar principle, hopefully with lessons learnt from history.** *John Scrace*

Above left: **The next batch of suburban units was constructed at Eastleigh from 1951 and was equipped with the then relatively new electro-pneumatic or 'EP' brake. Accordingly, their designation was 4-EPB. This system referred to the driver's operation of the braking system with the brakes still, of course, on the air system. The new control system was a success from the outset, allowing finer graduated control of the brakes, and these units became universally popular. Here, the first of the new 1951 units, then numbered S5001, is depicted at Wimbledon shortly before entering service. It still carries its original coach numbers following on from 4-SUB No 4754. These sets could also accelerate at a rate of 1mph per second up to 27mph. Compared with the 4-SUB suburban units, a route indicator blind is now fitted and buck-eye couplings have appeared. These were standardised from 5001.** *BR*

Below left: **The country end of the complex of junctions at Lewisham on 20 August 1955 sees a pair of 4-EPBs taking the line to Nunhead along the former South Eastern & Chatham lines. Here the railway diverged into a flyover and ground-level connections taking the routes to and from London Bridge as well as to Blackheath, Hither Green and Ladywell behind the photographer.** *Alan A. Jackson*

Above right: **A driving motor coach of penultimate Bulleid-design 4-EPB No S5259, No S14517S, is at London Bridge while on a Charing Cross to Dartford via Sidcup service on 5 February 1959.** *P. J. Sharpe*

Centre right: **Displaying a yellow warning panel on the blue livery (One of the earliest units to be painted blue), 4-EPB No 5219 enters New Malden station with the 12.52 Waterloo to Guildford via Cobham working on 4 February 1967.** *Stephenson Locomotive Society*

Right: **Against the buffers at Platform 5 of Waterloo, 4-EPB No 5227 awaits its next duty.** *Carl Symes*

Left: **A Charing Cross to Sevenoaks via Parks Bridge (avoiding Lewisham) and Orpington train, with 4-EPB No 5039 runs in to London Bridge. Unlike earlier SR electric units, provision has been made for electrical coupling up. With the decision made that double-deck operation was not to be proceeded with as a means of increasing capacity, the alternative of extending the length of trains from eight to ten cars was adopted and took place in stages from 1954 to 1957 — subject to necessary infrastructure alterations. This only applied to the former South Eastern services with two four-car sets now strengthened when necessary with a two-coach unit during peak periods.** *P. J. Sharpe*

Right: **A Wimbledon-Bognor Regis excursion at Raynes Park on 18 May 1959 with 4-EPB No S5148.** *J. H. Aston*

Below: **A favoured location for this photographer was Norwood Junction and here he captured an eight-car rake of suburban EPB units on a London Bridge to Tattenham Corner via Forest Hill and Norwood Junction working. The sets appear identical, although No S5247 leading has obviously received a more recent repaint.** *P. J. Sharpe*

Above: **Another 4-EPB eight-car formation, this time led by unit No S5236, is seen on either a Victoria to West Croydon via Streatham Hill and and Crystal Palace Low Level or Charing Cross to Sevenoaks via Swanley working.** *P. J. Sharpe*

Below: **A pair of the last two-car Bulleid units with new bodies built on SR-design NOL underframes, which appeared in 1959. Here, with No 5663 trailing, they depart Staines for Windsor, the line to Egham and Virginia Water diverging to the left.** *P. J. Sharpe*

Above: **In 1954, BR standard carriage designs began to be used for new electric stock, commencing that year with the first of the 2-EPB units intended for use on the South London lines, Wimbledon to West Croydon line and Eastern Section 10-car services. The first of the new BR standard design 2-EPB sets, No 5701 is depicted in March 1954. As with other SR third-rail units of the period, two 225hp English Electric traction motors were provided on each motor coach, but as this was a two-car unit, only one coach was powered. This was also the vehicle which contained the luggage compartment — seen left.** *BR*

Left: **In service this time, 2-EPB No 5701 enters Wandsworth Road on 12 May 1954 with the 2.17pm Victoria to London Bridge service running via the South London line. It will be noted that, as in the SR 4-EPB stock, access for the driver was through the guard's compartment rather than a separate door.** *J. H. Aston*

Left: **Mitcham station sees 2-EPB No 5712 on a West Croydon–Wimbledon service. This line owed its origins to the former LBSCR and formed an end-on connection with the LSWR at Merton Park. It now forms part of the Tramlink line.** *R. C. Riley*

Above: **London Bridge on 23 April 1958 is seen when it was the revised starting point for the 2.24pm Cannon Street to Dartford service, here led by 2-EPB No 5771. The service was scheduled to run via Lewisham and the Dartford loop line.** *J. H. Aston*

Right: **Another modification, and a former 2-EPB DTS is marshalled as part of DMU unit No 1202 as an intermediate TS. Note the additional jumper connections provided. The yellow warnings have also been painted out and any shoe gear recovered. It was photographed at Eastleigh depot on 7 July 1981.** *Colin J. Marsden*

Left: **Thirty-six 2-HAP units (two-car lavatory units with electro-pneumatic brake) were built, again at Eastleigh, in the period February–October 1958 (Nos-5601-36). These were completed using SR-built underframes. BR HAP units numbered 6001 onwards were on BR standard underframes. Here, one of the 5601 batch, No 5626 is depicted at Whitstable leading the 9.40am Charing Cross to Ramsgate service on 4 July 1959.** *J. H. Aston*

Above: **Men are seen walking with their backs to potential traffic at Hither Green in the early 1960s, with a train imminent, as per the signals, as 2-HAP No 5622 leads a 10-car formation London-bound past the motive power depot. Two new BRCW Type 3 diesel-electrics (later TOPS Class 33) can be seen in the background.** *P. J. Sharpe*

Left: **The BR-built 2-HAP units could accommodate a total of 138 passengers, 18 of whom were first class. No 5604 is at Ramsgate on 1 June 1959.** *J. Courtney Haydon*

Below: **By comparison, here is the original BR standard-design 2-HAP, No 6005. The driving trailer composite was almost identical to those supplied for the 'Hampshire' diesel-electric sets constructed at Eastleigh around the same time.** *BR*

Right: **Leading the 1.41pm Charing Cross to Gillingham service via Greenwich at London Bridge on 23 April 1958 is 2-HAP No 6014.** *J. H. Aston*

Right: **A pair of 2-HAP units on a westbound coastway working hold up work at Portfield Oil Terminal just east of Chichester. Unit No 6062 passes Class 33 diesel-electric No 33034 waiting in the sidings, on 13 May 1981. The crew standing by the ground frame is a feature often seen, but rarely recorded.** *Les Bertram*

Below: **The progress of electrification generally, together with increasing speeds and frequency of service, has meant routes once considered only suitable for main line stock are now given over to semi-suburban type working. One example is on the former SECR lines in Kent, and where for many years 2-HAP sets were used on local services. Here, set No 6066 trails a four-coach train leaving Canterbury East bound for Dover.** *P. J. Sharpe*

Below right: **Again at Canterbury East and with a Class 33 in the goods yard, 2-HAP No 6076 has just passed the rail-built starting signal and heads in the direction of Bekesbourne.** *P. J. Sharpe*

Left: **At Cannon Street, Saturday on 14 June 1969 the diverted 18.13 to Margate via Dover service has 2-HAP No 6151 leading the formation. The station is a sad shadow of its former glory.** *Stephenson Locomotive Society*

Below: **The former 2-HAP units (5601-36 series) with one coach having a lavatory were redesignated 2-SAP when the DTC was derated to second class only; No 5629 stands alongside 4-SUB No 4751 at Selhurst in October 1981.** *C. Burnham*

Left: **A former 2-HAP (BR standard) unit redesignated as 2-SAP, No 5904 is recorded leaving Staines on the 13.44 Windsor & Eton Riverside to Waterloo service on 1 September 1979.** *Les Bertram*

DEPARTMENTAL UNITS

Right: Following withdrawal from capital stock, it was long the practice of the Southern Region to utilise some vehicles in departmental use, and often as de-icing sets ready for winter. Here, renumbered de-icing unit No 95 was converted from two driving motors ex-Eastern Section 1925 stock. It was recorded in the coal sidings at Knights Hill on 14 September 1960 stabled en route from Stewarts Lane to Peckham Rye for electrical conversion. *R. C. Riley*

Above: A brief extension of life for a driving trailer from a former suburban unit: Instruction Unit No 055 at Fratton depot on 23 September 1984. *Chris Wilson*

Right: Ex-2-HAL de-icer No 001 (temporarily formed with a 2-EPB motor coach is seen at Shepperton). In its new role, the front end has been repainted, although unless cleaned regularly it will soon take on the appearance of that in the next view.
Ian Allan library

Left: **A pair of motor coaches from 2-HAL units are seen here on Sandite duties at East Grinstead on 23 November 1985. One member of staff from Eastleigh recalls working on these units which were lit internally by bulbs wired in series powered from the live rail. He recalls the flashes to be seen when attempting to replace a blown bulb were better than any Christmas lights!** *Alex Dasi-Sutton*

Below left: **An earlier internal use conversion, numbered 023 in the Departmental series and designated a 'Service Unit', is captured at Brighton on 14 May 1978.** *C. Burnham*

Winter Weather

By far the largest file of the three miscellaneous documents known to have survived (so far as the quantity of papers is concerned) is the most recent. Commencing with a report of 8 November 1956 it deals with the problem of winter weather and the effect of ice forming on conductor rails. Clearly, this was an ongoing problem and the decision was taken at this time to fit 'Ice scraper gear' to the tenders of eight 'C' class steam locomotives, which could be removed when not required. This equipment was air operated and hence the engines selected were all Westinghouse brake equipped. An air pressure of 90psi, controlled by a handle on the tender, raised or lowered the scraper into position, which was held in the scraping position by the air supply. In case of failure the scraper could be raised manually and secured out of use with a locking pin.

What may be obvious now was that any ice clearance would be not only required over actual running routes but also in the various electrified sidings used for stabling stock and a list of these locations, covering all three divisions of the Southern Railway, was appended. There followed almost immediately a special instruction on the operation of the steam engines which had been so fitted. The instruction, though, seemed to contradict the whole question of the 'priority' clearance, for it continued: '. . . the engines with the Ice Scraper Equipment fitted must be confined to electrified running lines and must not be permitted to run or be shunted on non-electrified lines, nor on sidings, electrified or otherwise. The engines performing the scraping will run "light" and will operate with the current on or off the conductor rail.'

Later, the instruction was amended so that an engine with a scraper could be shunted '. . . in the case of emergency only, with extreme caution and at dead slow speed' into a non-electrified siding.

Such arrangements eventually appeared in the sectional appendices in January 1960, although it was to be a short-lived enterprise as all eight steam engines were withdrawn by May 1962.

Above: **Proving it was not necessarily just the oldest units that were converted for internal use, a pair of 1949 4-SUB unit cars are seen at Wimbledon Park on 7 September 1977 displaying Departmental unit No 004. The weakness of all the suburban units in public service was their bogie design as it could give a poor passenger ride at any reasonable speed.** *John Scrace*

Below: **The Departmental sets were also used on 'Enparts' duties such as here with No 019 (ex-2SAP No 5629) approaching Winchester on the down main line on 15 April 1985 with a Slade Green to Eastleigh stores working.** *Colin J. Marsden*

BR MAIN-LINE AND SEMI-FAST UNITS

Left: By the 1950s, Southern Region management had decided that future main-line units should follow the basic principle of four- or two-car formations. It was not until 1956 that the first of the next generation of main-line units appeared. Enter, then, the CEP and BEP units — the BEPs differing from the four-car corridor 4-CEPs only in so far as one of the vehicles contained a buffet, although initially 7001/2 ran as three-car units until the buffet cars were delivered. Numbered in the 7001–7022 series for the BEP units and 7101 to 7204 for the CEP units, they were the mainstay of the Kent Coast electrification scheme in the late 1950s. No 7008 is seen at Whitstable in all-over green livery. These sets could accelerate at a rate of 0.75mph per second to 12mph and then at the slightly reduced rate of 0.56mph up to 50 mph. Roller bearings were fitted to the wheelsets of all the units from Nos 7003 and 7105 onwards. The green livery suited the trains well and this was of course the livery inherited from the Southern Railway and adopted by BR in 1948 as the standard for the Region's EMUs. The Southern's shade of green differed from that used on other regions until 1965. *P. J. Sharpe*

Left: The interior of an open second class saloon motor coach from a BEP/CEP unit. The distinctive features of Mk1 design are immediately apparent together with the fact that as this was main-line stock it meant the seating was 2+2 and not 3+2. As can be seen, the lighting is by traditional 24V ceiling lamps, although side reading lamps are also fitted. From unit No 7105 the control gear on the CEP/BEP units was altered and instead of EP control this was now oil/air camshaft switches. The brake gear was redesigned and changes were made to the bogies. Despite being three tons heavier at 43 tons per motor coach, the revised units had a slightly improved acceleration rate. *BR*

Above: **A trailer composite vehicle in each unit afforded accommodation in traditional compartments, one of which in the second class portion of a few coaches had a fully opening window to afford admittance of a stretcher passenger. This was as per contemporary Mk1 practice but the facility was little used and later-built electric stock did not continue this feature. Commonwealth bogies were fitted to later units which achieved the object of reducing the number of complaints about poor riding.** *BR*

Above: **A publicity view of the interior of a CEP/BEP unit. The photograph was taken to show the new Kent Coast units with Trojan moquette, although some photo retouching appears to have taken place. Notice the SR electric locomotive No 20003 in the background. These sets were given a further lease of life with overhaul and refurbishment at Swindon between 1979 and 1984.** *BR*

Right: **Leading a 12-coach rake near Meopham with a Kent Coast service is No 7139. Introduced in all-over green livery — front end included — the 4-CEP BR Mk1 design presented a pleasing appearance when painted in this way.** *BR*

Left: **Trailer composite No S70290 from a Kent Coast unit, with first class accommodation nearest the camera, shows the wider window spacing for such passengers. It was at this end too that the lavatory was installed. Phase 1 of what was the Kent Coast electrification scheme was approved by the British Transport Commission in February 1956 and covered the lines Gillingham-Faversham-Ramsgate, Faversham-Dover, and Sittingbourne-Sheerness, a total of 78 route miles.** *P. J. Sharpe*

Below: **The corridor side of a trailer composite, No S70333 illustrates the four doors provided, compared with three on the opposite side.** *P. J. Sharpe*

Left: **New CEP units are seen on trial at Wallington on 15 January 1959. Before being used on the Kent Coast these units were trialled on the Central Division in 1958-9. When taking up regular working these sets would spell the end of regular steam-hauled services and resulted in the cascading of steam motive power westwards to the South Western Division and the scrapping of the rest.** *John L. Smith*

Above: **This trailer second is from a 4-CEP unit of the later build and is seen at Ashford. These units are easily identified as they have Commonwealth bogies which, although heavier, gave a much better ride than the standard Mk1 bogie fitted to the original units.** *P. J. Sharpe*

Left: **Running on original bogies, 4-CEP No 7141 is seen on Central Division duties at Haywards Heath. These units acted initially as temporary replacements for the 6-PUL units which were then undergoing modifications as components were being altered. The unit is likely to be running to or from pre-1959 storage on the Ardingly branch.** *P. J. Sharpe*

Left: **4-CEP unit No 7195 is at Canterbury East. Phase 2 of the Kent Coast modernisation scheme in 1962 saw Sevenoaks-Tonbridge-Ashford-Folkestone-Dover-Deal-Ramsgate, Maidstone East-Ashford, Maidstone West-Paddock Wood, Canterbury West-Ramsgate, and Folkestone Harbour-Folkestone Junction electrified — a total of 132 route miles.** *P. J. Sharpe*

Above: **Brand-new 4-CEP No 7102 is on a test run from Selhurst to Three Bridges and is seen passing Redhill on 23 May 1956. The BR crest appears only on the driving motors.** *G. Daniels*

Below: **Photographed from the signalbox steps at London Bridge, 4-CEP No 7144 departs with the 9am service to Brighton on 13 May 1959. In the background, right, is a 4-SUB unit.** *J. H. Aston*

Above: **The 10.40am Victoria to Ramsgate near Beckenham Hill on 21 April 1963, at the head of which is 4-CEP No 7115 with the service diverted via the Catford Loop owing to engineering work.** *John Scrace*

Below: **In service on the Central Division, at Dorking North, is 4-CEP No 7209 heading the 12-car 09.18 Victoria to Portsmouth Harbour service on 8 August 1964.** *John Scrace*

Left: **Catering within a Kent Coast unit at a time when food was prepared and not just pre-packaged and then reheated.** *GEC*

Below: **A new departure in connection with the Kent Coast electrification was the building of 10 motorised luggage vans (MLV) at Eastleigh in the period 1959-61. These were to supplement the luggage capacity of the new Kent Coast EMUs when operating on boat train duties and weighed in at a hefty 47 tons. They were electrically compatible with the various EP-braked stock. They also possessed a battery-driven generator so they could be used on non-electrified dock lines if required. No 68005 was recorded at Stewarts Lane depot on 20 July 1963.** *J. H. Aston*

Above right: **The main use of the MLVs was on boat train services making the formation length 13 vehicles. An example of this is seen passing Canterbury East for Dover as an unidentified example of the type brings up the rear of the service.** *P. J. Sharpe*

Centre right: **In a reverse role, another MLV is seen leading an up service through the maze of pointwork at Ashford. The track branching to the right is for Appledore, Rye and Hastings.** *P. J. Sharpe*

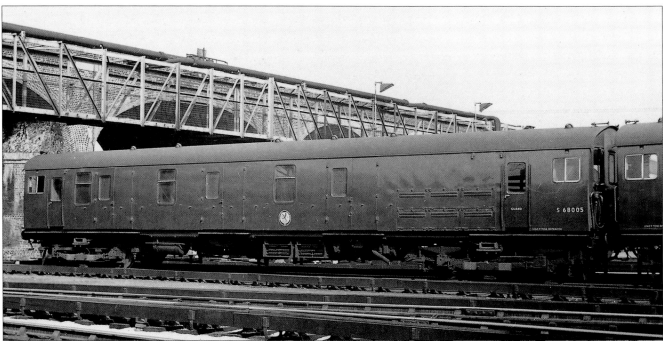

Right: **In revised and what was affectionately known as 'Jaffa Cake' orange and grey livery, MLV No 68007, renumbered 9007, waits at Platform 9 of London Bridge on 12 March 1988. By this time, dwindling needs for additional luggage accommodation had meant a new use had to be found for the vehicles and this came in parcels and mail work, mostly operating singly but capable of hauling a limited trailing load if required. All have now been withdrawn, with several surviving in preservation.** *Chris Gammell*

Above: **Having proved their worth on the Kent Coast lines, the CEP/BEP's design concept was taken one stage further in 1964 with the introduction of the CIG and BIG units for use on the Brighton line. The CIG/BIG units marked a major traction equipment departure by the SR. All traction motors were mounted on a non-driving motor coach and all driving cars were trailers. The reason was said to be that putting all the motors on one car impaired riding of the whole unit. Again, the 'B' referred to buffet facilities while the 'IG' was the telegraphic code for Brighton. These units were built at York, as Eastleigh had ceased new carriage building in 1963. Seen brand new and with a yellow panel from the outset, 4-CIG No 7301 awaits duty soon after delivery.** *Ian Allan Library*

Left: **The CIG and BIG units were among the last new stock to be built based on the Mk1 body shell, albeit with certain modifications, some at the suggestion of the BR Design Panel. One of these involved the corridor connections which included a more rigid design of bellows as well as wider ends, although draughts between sets persisted. Another change was the inset for the jumper cables on the front ends. In many respects this was a marked improvement between the vehicles making up each set. This combination is part of set No 7301 recorded at Waterloo on 1 October 1964.** *J. Courtney Haydon*

Left: The BIG sets were numbered in the 70xx series following on from the BEP sequence. The buffet can be seen as the third vehicle of set No 7034 passing Clapham Junction on a Brighton to Victoria working. Notice the position of the driver's 'Bardic' handlamp in the cab window. *Carl Symes*

Right: The first buffet vehicle, No S69301, for a 4-BIG unit (No 7031), seen at Victoria on 26 July 1965. A new system for passengers to identify vehicle accommodation was introduced by means of coloured coding and this is shown here with a red stripe by the cantrail of the buffet car, while yellow was used for first class. *John A. Upton Woods*

Left: At speed near Purley Oaks 4-CIG No 7301 leads a 12-coach formation, probably in the period 1965/6. In appearance these units indicated the shape of things to come as just a year or so later the REP and VEP units and TC trailer sets were introduced for the Bournemouth line. But, and as shown later, the REP and TC stock were mainly converted to locomotive-hauled coaches rather than totally new stock. *S. W. Stevens-Stratten*

This page: **As mentioned previously, another variant affecting the CIG and BIG stock compared with the Kent Coast design was the bogies, while another innovation was the position of the traction motors, which for the first time were carried on the bogies underneath the non-driving motor brake second. Seen in the first of three views** *(above)* **are the original and modified BR B5(S) type bogie as fitted to the intermediate trailers, and in the second** *(centre)* **the driving vehicles (DTC No S76741 of 4-CIG No 7391). The third view** *(below)* **shows the powered non-driving motor brake second with the heavier Mk6 type, as on No S62379 of the same set.** *John H. Bird/David Brown (two)*

Left: **An advantage for the interested passenger was that when walking between units, it was possible to observe — and photograph — the driving controls. These were straightforward compared with steam and are, left to right: EP brake, horn, forward-reverse, and master control. They also had cab-to-guard phone, speedometer and brake pressure gauge (in later years). This is DTC No S76613 of 4-CIG No 7339, photographed at Waterloo on 9 September 1984.** *David Brown*

Right: **Electrification to Bournemouth was finally confirmed in 1964/5 and accordingly steps were taken to introduce new stock as quickly as possible. The main-line units will be discussed shortly, so here the focus is on the four-car outer suburban and main-line local units which appeared from 1966 onwards. Known as the VEP units (for 'vestibuled' EPBs), these were high-capacity trains capable of fast acceleration, although, as with all the EP stock, careless starting efforts could cause them to blow their various circuit breakers when drivers applied a bit too much power compared with what the traction motors could accommodate. Posed when brand new in the carriage sidings at Clapham Junction, 4-VEP No 7707 was one of the first batch, the driving trailers of which were built at BR's York Works and the intermediate motor and trailer coaches at BR's Derby Works.** *S. W. Stevens-Stratten*

Left: **New units of the same type continued to be delivered throughout 1968 and aside from their initial use on the Bournemouth line, there were soon sufficient to replace earlier units on the Central Section and then, later still, were used as additional stock on the Eastern Section. Here, three brand-new four-car VEPs, Nos 7748, 7745 and 7747, head south from the builder and are seen at Knebworth on 9 April 1968 behind BRCW Type 3 No D6594.** *D. Percival*

Above: The interior of the 4-VEPs was functional if plain compared with previous decades, but reflected the modern age. Extensive use of Warerite decorative laminate veneers was made in a number of patterns, namely, 'Snow White', 'Persian Blue Linen', 'Grey Moresco', and 'Grey Linen'. *Ian Allan Library*

Above: First class accommodation in the VEPs was in compartments, but with a single door per compartment as well as a corridor. The umbrella rack was also a feature that did not appear in second class. Having an individual door had its advantages, but also drawbacks, and many a grouchy comment was made when a shiny toe-cap was inadvertently scuffed. *BR*

Left: Second class accommodation with individual luggage racks and, in the main, 3+2 seating. The curtains were orange, but later these were removed, while it will be noted that most accommodation photographed was still in the then current 'smoking permitted' mode. *BR*

Right: Saturday, 8 July 1967 and 4-VEP No 7710 is seen at Pokesdown, just east of Bournemouth. As built the first sets had a small yellow panel, although this was changed to full yellow ends for newly built stock from the following year. *John H. Bird*

Above: **The driving trailer composite of 4-VEP unit No 7705 at Millbrook on 20 May 1967. Full electric services to Bournemouth commenced on 10 July 1967, but in the meantime there was a slow introduction of the new services both for crew training and as the new stock became available.** *John H. Bird*

Right: **The 4-VEPs took over stopping and some semi-fast services on the Bournemouth line, with their formation meaning there would never be restaurant or buffet facilities provided. In the rain at Millbrook on 20 May 1967, Nos 7705 and 7706 are photographed heading for Southampton, the first day EMUs had been seen in the area.** *John H. Bird*

Left: **Reflections at Pirbright Junction, and the point of divergence for the lines to Farnham and Alton from the main Bournemouth route as a first-series 4-VEP passes, which is still in possession of the cast BR double-arrow symbol with which the sets were provided when new.** *J. L. McIvor*

Centre left: **A new use for some VEP sets from the new Central Division timetable of 8 May 1978 was on the Gatwick Express service which involved modification of the seating accommodation to provide a greater luggage space. Redesignated 4-VEG, they were numbered 7901 to 7912 and No 7905 is seen in Gatwick Airport sidings on 15 May 1978. This was destined to be a short-lived operation as they were replaced by Class 73 electro-diesels and push-pull sets. In so far as the VEPs were concerned, this was just one of a number of variations affecting the type over the years and, as such, many lasted way beyond their allotted time and well into the present century with the last being withdrawn in 2005.** *C. Burnham*

Below left: **For main-line services to Bournemouth, four-car powered 'tractor' units known as REPs (restaurant EPBs) were introduced together with either one or two non-power four-car trailer sets, 4-TCs. These could either be pushed or pulled, the original intention being to propel to Bournemouth and have the powered unit leading on the return leg to Waterloo. For services beyond Bournemouth, to Poole and Weymouth, which was not electrified, diesel-electric Class 33 locomotives would haul the 4-TC portion of the train. Delivery of the REPs commenced early in 1966, although it was a close run thing to have sufficient stock ready for the introduction of the new timetable in July 1967. (This had already been put back a month, from June.) Indeed, the operators at one time tried to obtain a six-month extension of steam traction, through to the end of December 1967 as it was feared insufficient new stock would be to hand. Steam had been allowed to run down too much and so the SR was left with a decision, either have enough stock available, or nothing, to run the services. Here a test run is taking place through Micheldever on 18 March 1967 with 4-REP No 3003, the layout at the station having been simplified and resignalled from December 1966.**
Alastair McIntyre

Left: The external appearance of the new trains was very similar to the 1965/6 BIG and CIG stock, although there were detail differences on the door and window layouts. The unit formation reverted to earlier practice with the driving motor seconds flanking the trailer brake first and restaurant cars, unlike the BIG/CIG layout in which the two motor bogies were placed under the non-driving motor coach. On the 4-REPs the body shells of the brake firsts and restaurant cars were second-hand — conversions from existing Mk1 steam stock. The driving motors however were of a new build. Unit No 3001 is seen during testing on 7 March 1967. *BR*

Right: Externally, the 4-TC sets were similar but could quickly be identified as being non-powered as there was no shoe gear. Displaying the '91' headcode, this was a Bournemouth 'fast', calling at Southampton only. The timings were originally set as Southampton in 70 minutes and Bournemouth in 100 minutes for the fast services, although given a clear route this was easily adhered to and 60 minutes to Southampton was not uncommon. A 12-car working with 4-TC No 422 leading approaches Brookwood en route from Bournemouth to Waterloo. *BR*

Left: A 4-REP, No 3007, leads a pair of 4-TCs into Southampton with a down service in June 1967, with the former power station — now replaced by a shopping complex — on the right. Long considered a bottleneck, Southampton now has reversible working through the tunnel which, since the days of MAS, has seen regular use.
John H. Bird

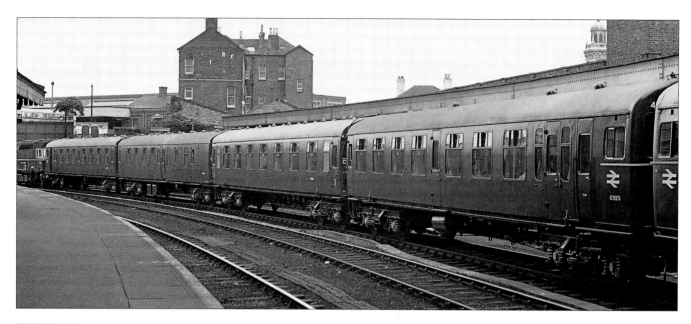

Above: **As previously mentioned, from Bournemouth the last section of line to Weymouth was initially worked by diesel traction. A number of Type 3 (later Class 33) diesel-electric locomotives were made compatible for working in multiple with the EP-braked REP/TC/VEP units. This scene was recorded in June 1967 during crew training at Bournemouth and with No D6525 attaching itself to a pair of 4-TCs with No 405 leading, in the centre through roads at Bournemouth Central.** *John H. Bird*

Left: **Compatibility verified at St Denys on a very wet 9 August 1966. A new 4-TC set is hauled north by Type 3 Bo-Bo No D6542, probably en route from Bournemouth to Eastleigh.** *John H. Bird*

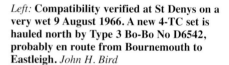

Left: **Some of the locomotive-hauled services were handed over to electric traction early. On 4 April 1966, just two days after electric units had taken over the Bournemouth-Waterloo working, 4-REP No 3003 is in charge at Totton, although for the time being sandwiched between two 4-TC sets, Nos 408 and 416.** *Alastair McIntyre*

Above: **Southampton on 10 September 1967 sees 4-REP No 3005 entering Platform 1 on an afternoon Waterloo service while a Class 73 'ED' waits in the sidings on the down side.** *Alastair McIntyre*

Above & left: **As with the 4-VEPs, the interior of the Bournemouth TC stock was functional and plain. Previous surveys had indicated a considerable number of passengers still preferred compartment stock and, accordingly, this was provided for both first and second classes. In décor though, apart from the obvious three-a-side compared with four-a-side seating, the only obvious differences between the classes was the provision of umbrella racks and armrests in first class.** *BR*

Left: **By comparison with the plain panelling within the compartments, the 4-REP refreshment vehicles incorporated veneer panelling as well as loose seating. As ever, though, there was also a trade-off — making passengers too comfortable meant they would monopolise the area for too long, so restricting the access of others. Here at least, all appear to be partaking of slightly more than just a single cup of tea — aren't the fashions wonderful as well!**
Ian Allan Library

Right: **Corridor brake second No S70815 of 4-TC No 404 is recorded at Bournemouth. As built, all the REP and TC sets displayed all-over plain blue livery, shortly changed to blue and grey, and green was never carried.**
John H. Bird

Above: **A brand-new open second from a 4-REP or 4-TC driving trailer in which it appears the ceiling bulbs have yet to be added. Second class seating here was always 2+2 and although relatively comfortable, these sets could be noisy and prone to draughts.**
Ian Allan Library

Above: **The corridor connections between 4-TC sets (and REP-TC) followed the same styling as that of the CIG and BIG units and were reasonably draught-free for the first few years of life. Unfortunately, by the end of the 1970s these units were beginning to show signs of the tremendous wear they experienced on daily trips up and down to Bournemouth and the area near the connections between coaches was rarely a place where standing passengers would loiter by choice.**
John H. Bird

Left: **On the four-track section west of Southampton No 302, one of the three short-lived 3-TC sets (unit Nos 301-303) leads an 11-coach rake eastwards on 8 February 1969. The funding of the Bournemouth electrification scheme was so tight that a logical complement of complete four-coach TC sets could not be afforded. In addition, it was originally considered necessary to have a few 3-TC sets for Southampton Docks (which closed to passenger trains shortly afterwards). The '91' headcode indicates the service is Southampton and Waterloo only.** *John H. Bird*

Right: **A new 4-TC set, No 409, is seen at Basingstoke on 24 September 1966 during a test working. As was standard, both buck-eye and conventional coupling hooks were provided with a screw coupling safely secured in the guard's compartment of each set. Note also the conventional tail lamp.** *M. Pope*

Left: Crew training and familiarisation of the new Bournemouth line stock involved men from a number of depots, although principally these were from Waterloo, Eastleigh and Bournemouth. Here, such a training run with 4-REP No 3001 and 4-TCs Nos 402 and 404 from Basingstoke to Bournemouth is seen passing an electricity sub-station near Shawford Junction on 18 March 1967 and showing the new connection, installed into the down relief line just a few months earlier. *John H. Bird*

Left: Breaking new ground on a visit to the remains of the Kemp Town branch (by then goods only) at Brighton on 22 September 1967, No 422 is temporarily reduced to a three-car unit. The occasion was Southern Counties Touring Society's 'South Eastern Rambler' with Type 3 'Crompton' No D6529 providing the motive power. *John Vaughan*

Right: Platform 1 at Southampton — the 'Central' suffix being dropped 1967-94, following closure of 'Terminus' station. On 9 March 1968, 4-REP No 3001 leads a semi-fast service which will call at Southampton Airport, Eastleigh, Winchester, Basingstoke, Woking and Waterloo. These services required much harder running on the part of the crews to maintain the timings and it appears the driver is anxious to get away! *John H. Bird*

Left: The electric service to Bournemouth from Southampton was 10 minutes faster than the previous best steam timings, although to be fair, loads were predictable and some speed restrictions had been eased. One big advantage of the new traction was the removal of the fire risk in places such as the New Forest. Here, 4-REP No 3006 heads a Bournemouth-bound service near Beaulieu Road station, unusually with the powered set leading in this direction of travel. *John Vaughan*

Above: Clapham Junction in the post steam era, on 18 September 1974, but with almost all the stock visible now consigned to history. Forming the 10.38 Weymouth-Waterloo 4-REP No 3006 leads 4-TC sets Nos 408 and 417 passing between two members of the short-lived Class 74 electro-diesel type, Nos 74003 and 74004. *Brian Morrison*

Right: The driving end motor bogie of DMS No S62141 of 4-REP No 3001, is seen at Waterloo on 9 September 1984. *David Brown*

Left: **The old with what was then the new. 'Nelson' 4-COR No 3136 and 4-TC No 414 at Waterloo on 27 December 1969. The contrast in styling is obvious and so it should be, with 30 years separating the designs. Notice the side destination boards on the TC which was a concept reintroduced back in 1946. A similar contrast would be provided today if a 4-TC were lined up alongside one of the latest units from the 21st century, but of course, nothing is permanent and styles and appearances change, even if these are so subtle they are not at first noticed. The 4-CORs disappeared in the early 1970s, the 4-REPs and TCs less than 20 years later. There was a proposal to retain a limited number of REPs but re-formed to six cars without restaurant facilities and, indeed, trials with at least one of these did take place. It was not to be, and bouncy push-pull to Bournemouth was relatively short-lived, perhaps little different really to memories of the 4-CORs!** *J. Rickard*

Above: **An unique locomotive-hauled set No 900 formed from electric stock in May 1963, specifically for use on the diesel-electric (D65xx) locomotive-hauled 5.20pm London Bridge to Tunbridge Wells West via Oxted service. The seven-coach train comprised the demotored motor brake coach from 2-BIL No 2006, two 10-compartment six-a-side compartment trailer seconds, a nine-compartment trailer composite, two more 10-compartment trailer seconds, and the driving trailer from No 2006. The trailer seconds came from withdrawn 4-SUBs in the 'augmented' series, the trailer composite was originally designed as such but used as a third/second since new in 1946, and was given first-class seats for its brief new life. The set was formed because of a desperate need for electrically heated stock on the Oxted line as steam locomotives were being withdrawn.** *Ian Allan Library*